D0506725

LEADERSHIP UNDER FIRE!

From the Battlefield to Corporate America

By

**Brigadier General Nick Halley
(U.S. Army, Retired)**

Attention–Professional Organizations, Corporations and Colleges: Quantity discounts are available on bulk purchases of this book. For more information please contact Nick Halley at 847-719-2637 or www.generalnickspeaks.com

ACKNOWLEDGMENTS

My deepest thanks to the following people and organizations:

The United States Military Academy at West Point, NY, where I learned honor and integrity, and where I developed as a man, leader, and soldier

The United States Army and all the nameless soldiers who accepted me as their leader during both peace-time and war in over 30 years of active service.

The 82nd Airborne Division – the best fighting unit in the Armed Forces of the U.S. – the heart and soul of my military career.

The officers I have served with – especially in the Airborne (paratrooper) organizations – who are life-long friends, fellow soldiers and great leaders.

To my family, who have supported me through good and bad times.

The many people in the National Speakers Association (NSA) – Illinois Chapter who provided help and encouragement every step of the way. Special thanks to Kevin O'Connor, the current President of the NSA-IL, who has been a mentor and friend.

DEDICATION

To my son, Matthew Nicholas Halley, who
is the light of my life and my inspiration.
No man has ever had a better son.

CONTENTS

ACKNOWLEDGMENTS iii

PREFACE xi

Chapter 1: Key Leadership Observations 1

Chapter 2: Leadership vs. Management 15

Chapter 3: Leadership Types and Traits 19

Chapter 4: The Importance of Listening 27

Chapter 5: Choosing the Best 35

Chapter 6: Power and Ego 43

Chapter 7: Being a Good Follower 55

Chapter 8: Leading by Example 63

Chapter 9: Providing Vision 77

Chapter 10: Saying "No" to the Status Quo 83

Chapter 11: Balancing Caring and Compassion 91

Chapter 12: Making Decisions on Limited Information 99

Chapter 13: Right Unless Proven Wrong   107

Chapter 14: Building on Strengths   113

Chapter 15: Beware of "Yes" People   123

Chapter 16: Lonely at the Top   127

Chapter 17: Leadership Challenges/Final   133
Observations

ABOUT THE AUTHOR   139

ORDER FORM   141

Brigadier General Nick Halley

Nick Halley – 1945

Cadet Halley at West Point Graduation

Colonel Halley at 82nd Airborne Division Review

**Col Halley, General Hosmer, Colin Powell
At National Defense University**

General Halley with Korean Chief of Staff

PREFACE

"To command is to serve,
Nothing more and nothing less."
Andre Malraux
Man's Hope

This book is for people who want to become better leaders. It's intended to teach, motivate, and inspire leaders at all levels to take immediate action in their organizations to become more effective leaders. My leadership background includes West Point, more than thirty years of active military duty, and vice president and general management positions in the corporate world.

These experiences, plus stressful combat leadership responsibilities and exposure to a multitude of other leaders, varying from commissioned officers to corporate executives, have inspired me to formulate my own theories on leadership. These theories combine combat-tested military leadership principles with corporate leadership principles and experiences.

Leadership is an art rather than a science. This book is not a "cookbook" that provides specific "recipes" to make you a leader, nor is it a "how-to" book that gives you specific steps to take in a specific order to become a good leader. Leadership cannot be illustrated by charts and diagrams with arrows pointing in various directions.

The first three chapters in the book are a background or basis for my leadership beliefs. Chapters 4-16 provide specific principles derived from first-hand leadership experiences, rather than academic theories.

Chapter 17 provides some final leadership thoughts, observations, and challenges.

Academic approaches to leadership are fine, but they fail to capture the "down and dirty" essence of true leadership under the most stressful conditions. The proven, time-tested principles discussed in this book must be applied to your particular situation, and consistent with your own personality and leadership style.

This book bridges the gap between the military and corporate worlds, and takes the best leadership practices from both sectors. It presents these principles in a clear and concise manner, with plenty of real world corporate and military "war stories" as examples.

I hope you enjoy the book. Be ready for a nonstandard and sometimes controversial discussion of leadership.

CHAPTER ONE

KEY LEADERSHIP OBSERVATIONS

*"When you've got a battle to win,
leadership determines the outcome."*
Nick Halley

Whether you're fighting on a battlefield, or operating in a corporate environment, leadership is the critical success factor. Leadership is even more important to the success of an organization than the skills and talents of the employees. This has been seen and proven in many sectors of our society, including sports, the military, and business.

For example, in the sports world, the coach is often just as important as the players in terms of wins and losses. A team of good players can lose game after game, season after season, under poor leadership. However, when an exceptional coach takes over, or they gain a new team leader, the same players normally start winning. This happens every year on some teams in the National Football League.

The same occurs in the military. When a military unit of any size needs improvement, a new effective leader can produce positive results almost overnight. I've also seen this happen time after time in the corporate world. An organization under poor leadership suffers, and eventually fails. However, the

1

same organization under a good leader can overcome challenges and make significant, positive changes in a short time with the same employees.

Consider the following question that's often used in military schools to highlight the importance of great leadership: Which opponent is more threatening, fifty lions led by one lamb, or fifty lambs led by one lion? The toughest opponent is clearly the group led by the lion. The lion will get the best efforts from the lambs and lead them to overcome many obstacles and successfully accomplish the required tasks. Teams with good individuals and a weak leader never reach their full potential.

Teams with good individuals and a weak leader never reach their full potential.

Although good teams are essential to any organization, they're not normally effective without good leadership. As a retired army officer, I hesitate to use a naval reference – but a ship with a great leader as captain is almost always a great ship, regardless of the quality of the individual crew members. Throughout history, the positive impact of great leaders on organizations is well documented. Leaders at all levels are in great demand in all sectors of our society. Unfortunately, I've found that the supply of qualified leaders is extremely limited and doesn't satisfy the great demand.

Several corporate surveys I've seen reveal that about seventy percent of employees aren't satisfied with their leaders. In these same surveys, about ninety percent of the leaders believe they're doing a good job in leading their employees. That's quite a disconnect, but in most cases the employees are probably right. These high numbers of dissatisfied employees are partially due to the fact that our workers rightly have a very high expectation of our leaders. We expect our leaders – at all levels – to be good leaders from day one, even if they're still in the learning stage of their leadership development.

Now compare these satisfaction levels with those in the military. Using the same surveys, only about fifteen percent of military personnel (versus seventy percent in the corporate world) were dissatisfied with their leaders. Granted, the corporate and military worlds are somewhat different. However, I've found that soldiers and civilian employees have very similar expectations of their leaders. In any case, a seventy percent dissatisfaction level in the corporate world is "light years" apart from the fifteen percent level in the military.

Why Is Corporate Leadership Dissatisfaction So High?

There are two reasons why the rate of leadership dissatisfaction exists at higher levels in the corporate environment than in the military environment. The first reason is the way people are selected for leadership positions, and the second is the quality and frequency of leadership training.

Basically, the military and corporate worlds often select people for leadership positions based on different criteria. In the military, it's based primarily on demonstrated leadership abilities and leadership potential, and not on achievements. It doesn't matter if a soldier can march better than anyone else, present great briefings, look sharp in uniform, or shoot weapons the best. The military chooses proven leaders who have the ability to motivate and inspire ordinary soldiers to accomplish extraordinary feats.

In the corporate world, my experience has been that leaders are chosen based primarily on achievement. For example, the best salesperson is often selected to be the sales manager – a difficult leadership position. Or the best engineer might be selected to lead the engineering organization. In many cases the person with the most seniority is selected to be the leader.

Clearly, the skills needed to be a good individual salesperson or engineer is very different from the leadership skills needed to head the organization.

Clearly, the skills needed to be a good individual salesperson or engineer is very different from the leadership skills needed to head the organization. In addition, longevity in an organization doesn't ensure that the person is a good leader. Oftentimes in these situations, the new leader lacks natural leadership skills, or sufficient leadership training and experience. This can, and usually does, cause profound leadership problems in the organization.

Another reason the military produces a larger percentage of effective leaders is the frequency and quality of leadership training. In the military, from day one, officers and NCOs (non-commissioned officers) receive extensive, continual, quality leadership training from people who are proven leaders.

For example, in Desert Storm, a month before I led more than 10,000 soldiers under my command into Iraq, I still received leadership training from my senior commanders. Almost every day, the field commanders received leadership bulletins and other pieces of information geared toward making us more effective leaders. We also received monthly face-to-face leadership training from our senior commanders.

This leadership training and the leadership bulletins continued to emphasis its importance, reinforced the leadership principles previously taught, and stressed the high level of responsibility of leaders. The frequency and quality of this training was very important. Our troops deserve great leadership. Bad leadership often translates into tragic and unnecessary casualties and defeat.

In the corporate world, however, I found that the quality and quantity of leadership training was insufficient. I saw many cases where newly assigned corporate executives were sent to one- or two-week leadership schools, and then declared to be "qualified leaders." Many of these classes were presented by instructors with great academic knowledge but no actual leadership experience. In addition, the frequency of follow-up classes was "hit and miss" at best.

Military vs. Corporate Leadership

One of my biggest surprises in the corporate world, after more than 30 years in the military, was that military leadership and corporate leadership are about ninety percent the same. The first major similarity is dealing with change. In combat, the rapidly changing and unpredictable battlefield conditions force leaders to quickly react to uncontrollable change.

Actual combat situations are always different than anticipated in the best plans. The weather and terrain may be rougher than expected. The enemy locations and numbers, as well as their reactions and tactics, are usually different than anticipated. Successful combat leaders must expertly adapt their battle plans instantly to adjust to the unexpected changes, or risk the lives of their soldiers.

Likewise, in the corporate world, leaders must quickly and effectively react to changing customer requirements, competitors' tactics and strategies, and the changing marketplace.

> *"Willingness to change is a strength,*
> *even if it means plunging part of the company*
> *into total confusion for awhile."*
> **Jack Welch, former General Electric CEO**

At the same time that leaders, corporate or military, are reacting to changes, they must also create change. Good leaders will sense weaknesses in the enemy, or in the market, or in the competition, and then initiate changes to take advantage of those opportunities. They might change tactics, develop a new advertising angle, or a more advanced product, or a more receptive customer service policy. Many leaders fail because they're unable to recognize the need for changes, or lack the courage to initiate the needed changes.

The second important similarity between military and corporate leadership involves people. People are the most important commodity in the military, as well as in the business world. Most companies don't like to admit the fact that, in reality, almost all products and services produced by their company are also produced – with equal or similar quality – by rival companies.

Many leaders fail because they're unable to recognize the need for changes, or lack the courage to initiate the needed changes.

You may think your organization has the highest quality products, or the best service, but that's not necessarily true. In most cases, other companies can do what you do just as well. Ultimately, the major difference between two rival organizations is the people who design, make, market, service, and sell your products or services. People are your most important product.

> *"People are like flowers. They are to be cultivated, and not to be destroyed."*
> **Jack Welch**

One of the first books required in military schools is the ancient Chinese philosopher Sun-tzu's *Art of War*.

In fact, some corporations have purchased copies for their executives because of the strong parallels between military and corporate leadership in preparing for and conducting "war." One passage describes the critical relationship between leaders and followers.

> *"Treat your soldiers like your own children and they will follow you to the deepest valleys."*
> **Sun-tzu**

An effective leader knows that the most important part of an army, or an organization, is the people involved. How they are treated and led will determine the effectiveness of the organization.

You can be the boss and give orders, but you won't be an effective leader unless your people accept you as their leader.

It's critical that your people recognize you as their leader. You can be the boss and give orders, but you won't be an effective leader unless your people accept you as their leader. It doesn't matter what position you hold, how big your office is, or how much money you make. If your team doesn't view you as their leader, your effectiveness will be severely limited.

The Military Can Learn from the Corporate World

The corporate world has two major leadership

advantages over the military. In the corporate world, a capable and accomplished leader can be advanced at a very fast rate. It's not unusual for a relatively young leader to be rapidly promoted to higher leadership positions over other leaders and managers who are much older and more experienced.

This system allows exceptional leaders to progress at a pace consistent with their abilities and accomplishments. It's very positive in an organization for the employees to feel their rate of advancement is based primarily on their demonstrated abilities, and not restricted by any predetermined timetable.

In the military, advancement can be slightly accelerated for exceptional performers, but promotions are greatly restricted by a predetermined timetable, based on total time in the military and time in the current grade/rank. Exceptional leaders often get frustrated and impatient as they see less capable (but qualified) leaders being promoted because of their seniority. This system causes numerous excellent leaders to leave the military service for the "greener pastures" in corporate America.

In corporate America, job descriptions can usually be altered to fit an employee's strengths and weaknesses. This results in greater employee satisfaction and increases the productivity of the organization.

In the military, the job descriptions are generally fixed. People are normally "forced" into these positions with relatively little flexibility in changing the job descriptions. In effect, this is sometimes akin to "forcing a square peg into a round hole." In many cases, this results in the loss to the organization of some very special talents.

"The discipline which makes the soldiers of a free country reliable in battle is not to be gained by harsh or tyrannical treatment. On the contrary, such treatment is far more likely to destroy than make an Army."
Major General John Schofield
Addressing the West Point Cadets, August 11, 1887

Harsh Treatment

Leaders don't need to use harsh treatment to enforce standards. I learned this when I was a Plebe (freshman) at West Point. During the Christmas break, my high-school girlfriend visited me at West Point. At that time, it was strictly forbidden to touch or even hold hands in public.

One day we were walking up a set of steps and I held her hand to steady her. I noticed that a West Point Tactical Officer was standing near the top of the steps and observed my actions. I knew I was in trouble. He asked to speak with me, but made sure the conversation took place some distance away from my girlfriend.

He quietly asked if I knew holding hands wasn't permitted. When I explained that I was helping my friend up the steps, he responded that the correct way was to have her hold my arm. He did report the incident and I did receive a punishment of a few demerits. However, I was impressed with how the officer had handled the situation. He enforced the rules and administered the appropriate punishment.

However, he did it in such a way that I was able to maintain my dignity. He also quietly instructed me on how I could have handled the situation differently without violating the rules. The lesson: you can maintain high standards, enforce rules, and make corrections without embarrassing or humiliating the offender. People respect leaders who maintain high standards, and they normally won't resent being corrected if it's done in a professional manner.

Determine Your Critical Success Factors

The final key factor in effective leadership is the ability to maintain focus and prevent distractions from interfering with success. In the military, I learned the critical success factor theory. This powerful concept doesn't require tons of paperwork or time. It's a simple exercise that helps leaders focus their time on the critical issues.

To determine your own critical success factors, make a list of the three to six most critical tasks you must accomplish to be successful in your job. Write each critical item down in a bullet format. Review them with your supervisor and refine your list, based on that interaction. Post your list at your desk in a visible spot.

Each day, before leaving your office, look over the critical success factors and determine whether or not you spent your valuable time that day on the items on your list. Did you spend your time on your critical success factors, or did you allow yourself to get distracted? Distraction is sometimes inevitable, but it's important that you discipline yourself to spend your time on your critical success factors and not on the "emergency of the day." Over time, you'll gradually see that you're spending more time on these items that produce success, and less time on the ones that divert your attention.

Leadership Warnings

Two cautions: first, remember the importance of teamwork. Everyone must work together as a team toward a common goal. However, every team needs strong leadership to define the team goals and keep the team focused on those goals. The leader must also listen to the team members and ultimately make decisions that support the accomplishment of the overall team goals.

When a committee of people lead the team, rather than an individual, the team will not normally be effective. Committees tend to collapse under internal conflict and, instead of making the best decisions; they make decisions that satisfy the greatest number of team members.

The second caution involves the dilution of responsibility and authority. I once had a boss who said that if it took more than five seconds to answer the question, who's responsible, and who has the authority to make a decision on a given issue, then the organization's in trouble. I've often asked that question in the corporate world and sometimes received a thirty-minute answer.

One of the main military principles of war is "Unity of Command." That means some specific individual must ultimately be in charge and responsible. Beware of leaders who appear strong, but blur the lines of authority and responsibility to the point where you become unsure who's in charge of what, or who the responsible person is.

As an example of this dilution, consider the matrix management system. While this well-known management technique provides a sound system of checks and balances, it greatly dilutes the lines of responsibility and makes it very difficult to answer the question: "Who's in charge of what and who's responsible for what?"

One common variety of the matrix management system is an organization with regional general managers and functional managers. The regional managers integrate and optimize all functions in their regions and form an effective regional team responsive to the regional customers.

The functional managers are responsible for their function throughout all the regions. For example, in an engineering company, these functions could be installation, systems engineering, project management, warehouse operations, etc. The matrix management system depends on the two managers working together to make decisions, solve problems, and develop strategy.

However, the regional manager is trying to optimize operations in his or her region, and the functional manager is trying to optimize his or her function throughout the organization. These different goals normally conflict. Given a particular issue or problem, who's ultimately responsible and who has the authority: the regional or functional manager?

This system often leads to confusion on the part of the workers (who's the boss?), split loyalties, different priorities, and slower decision times, because of the need to coordinate major decisions with a broader group of people.

Senior managers who are most comfortable with blurred lines of authority and shared responsibility embrace the matrix management system. Many executives also like this system because they prefer systems with blurred lines of responsibility. Beware of these types of people.

CHAPTER TWO

LEADERSHIP VS. MANAGEMENT

"There is a difference between leadership and management. Leadership is of the spirit, compounded of personality and vision – its practice is an art. Management is of the mind, more a matter of accurate calculations, statistics, methods, timetables, and routine – its practice is a science. Managers are necessary; leaders are essential."
British General Sir William Slim
of World War II Fame

So what's the difference? Essentially, you lead people, and you manage things.
Another view is:
"Management is doing things right; Leadership is doing the right things."
Peter F. Drucker

Consider the following definitions of leadership and management:

Leadership:
- The art of influencing and directing people to accomplish their mission.
- Persuading ordinary people to perform in extraordinary ways.

- Getting someone to do something you want done because he or she wants to do it.

Management:
- Solves problems, fixes processes, avoids conflicts, allocates resources, and ensures orderly results.

In short, managers are problem solvers focused on resources, organization, and stated goals. They're concerned with systems and processes, control, directing, and improving efficiency. Managers keep the work on-track and supervise details. Managers are concerned with people as resources – making sure the correct number and type of person are assigned to the various tasks.

> **"Don't bring me any more definitions of leadership. I don't know what the definition is, but I know a leader when I see one."**

Leadership is a quality in someone that can be identified, but not always defined. Even experienced military officers have difficulty in defining leadership and what makes a person a leader. I observed a high ranking general in Operation Desert Storm preparing to present a leadership class to other officers.

A staff officer was helping the general choose one of the many definitions of leadership for use in the class. The staff officer kept bringing different definitions to the general for his approval, but the general kept rejecting them. Finally losing his patience, he told the staff officer, "Don't bring me any more definitions of leadership. I don't know what the definition is, but I know a leader when I see one."

I think we all know a good leader when we see one. If you look at any third-grade class, or any team, or any group, you can identify the leader. Just watch the interaction of the group. Who are the members of the group looking to for direction? Whose ideas are they following? Who is influencing the group's actions? The identification of the leader

The future of any organization depends on its future leaders.

will be obvious. Incidentally, the person theoretically in charge or doing the most talking isn't necessarily the real leader of the group.

What does a leader do?
- Selects and develops people, and other leaders.
- Motivates people.
- Develops goals and visions, and then effectively communicates them to everyone in the organization.
- Produces change, and sets the direction for change.
- Takes personal responsibility for action and results.

Perhaps the most important task a leader performs is to identify and develop other leaders. Jack Welch, the former CEO of General Electric, said:

"It's not a leader's job to develop followers, but to develop other leaders."
Jack Welch

The future of any organization depends on its future leaders. We're all going to eventually retire, move to another position or leave the company. Therefore, the development of our successors is critical to the organization. In the military, commanders are praised and held in high esteem based on the leaders they develop. In the corporate world – in many cases – leaders are reluctant to develop leaders because they don't want to create competitors for their positions.

A final note: A person can be both a great leader and great manager but, based on my experience, it's rare. Managers and leaders are usually very different types of people. It's key to remember, however, that both leaders and managers are absolutely essential to an organization.

CHAPTER THREE

LEADERSHIP TYPES AND TRAITS

"Leaders come in many forms, with many styles and diverse qualities. There are quiet leaders and leaders one can hear in the next county. Some find strength in eloquence, some in judgment, some in courage."
John W. Gardner

The U.S. Army has conducted many studies over the years to determine exactly what traits and personality types make great leaders. They anticipate that if they could only find the right formula, the right combination of traits, they could more easily develop and train the great number of leaders needed in our Army.

The problem, however, is that no matter how many studies you conduct, or how closely you study military leaders through history, no perfect or consistent set of characteristics exists. No specific personality types become the best leaders. Good leaders come in all forms, sizes, shapes and personality types. Most leaders can be categorized as one of the following types. Some leaders change their basic style from time-to-time based on specific situations.

Types of Leaders
Inspirational
Charismatic
Coercive
Manipulative
Value-Led

Great leaders exist under each type. Many great leaders are combinations of the types listed above. History is full of examples. Some examples of great inspirational and charismatic leaders include:

No matter how many studies you conduct, or how closely you study military leaders through history, no perfect or consistent set of characteristics exists. No specific personality types become the best leaders.

Rudolph Giuliani, the Mayor of New York City during the September 11th attacks; Winston Churchill, the wartime leader of England; and Martin Luther King, Jr., the famous civil rights leader.

The most influential inspirational and charismatic leader in my life was General Carl Vuono, who was my commander in the 82nd Airborne Division Artillery, and later became the Army Chief of Staff.

Such leaders inspire their followers to accomplish great things. They're able to tap into the emotions of the followers and make them believe in and want to accomplish the goals set by the leaders because they're worthwhile and noble. People work hard for these leaders because they don't want to let them down. The followers strongly feel the leaders deserve their support.

Some great value-led leaders are General Omar Bradley from World War II, the great leader Mahatma Gandhi from India, and Mother Teresa. They motivated followers because of the respect and reverence they inspired. Followers feel value-led leaders are great men or women who truly are leaders of a great cause or movement, and have an almost mystical sense of doing the right things.

Coercive leaders and manipulative leaders are not necessarily fun to work for, but they can be very effective in the short term. Some notable examples are Genghis Kahn, and General George Patton. These leaders were effective due to the strength of their personalities and the force of their wills. In many cases, they motivated people by fear, but were still very effective leaders.

Understand that you can also learn great lessons from bad leaders. Under such a leader, you can clearly see and experience the bad results and missed opportunities that prevail. You tend to remember these bad experiences and guard against making the same mistakes when you're in a leadership position.

We're all going to encounter bad leaders in our careers. It's important to realize that the leadership situation will eventually change, so don't get discouraged, but keep doing your job. Don't allow bad leaders to make you do bad things.

In my career, I've encountered a few bad leaders but, fortunately, most of my experience has been with good ones. The great leaders in my past influenced me in many positive ways. Previously, I mentioned General Carl Vuono, from the 82nd Airborne Division Artillery. He taught me a leader can be firm and demanding, and yet maintain high standards and strict discipline.

I also greatly admire Major General Vernon Lewis and Major General Ed Trobaugh. General Lewis was a great Division Artillery commander who inspired everyone to do their best. He strongly maintained high standards, but he led by example all the time.

General Trobaugh was the 82nd Airborne Division commander during the invasion of Grenada. He had great physical and moral courage. He made many tough decisions during the Grenada operation that were not always politically correct, but were the right things to do. As a result, his career was possibly damaged, but he always had the courage to put his career second and the welfare of his men and the mission first.

Lieutenant General Gary Luck, my boss in the first Gulf War, commanded the 18th Airborne Corps during Desert Storm. He was a very effective value-led type leader, who instilled confidence in everyone. He was a leader who picked the right people for the right jobs and then let them do their jobs with minimum interference. He was always there when you needed him for advice and guidance but he clearly believed "his" commanders would do the right things at the right times.

Jack Scanlon from Motorola was also a great charismatic leader. He inspired confidence with his own work ethic and great knowledge. He was a good listener who instinctively knew what to do and when to do it.

Leadership Traits

All leaders possess certain leadership traits. And while all leaders have these traits, they possess them in different quantities. Consider the following 10 essential traits:

1. Character

Behavior is an indication of character. Leaders must distinguish those things which are right and those which are wrong. It requires strength of character to meet a difficult situation head-to-head and not avoid unpleasant situations or pass the problem to someone else.

> **People with character attract followers; those with a lack of character repel followers.**

People with character attract followers; those with a lack of character repel followers.

2. Integrity

Strong character and high moral principles. Being truthful, honest and forthright all the time. Being committed to the highest moral, ethical, and professional standards. Integrity is the foundation of building trust. No one can take away your integrity – only you can give it away.

3. Values

Your attitude about people, concepts, or things defines your values. A person with good values chooses getting the job done over money, prefers self-satisfaction over getting credit for a success, and gives credit to the team.

4. Teamwork

Leaders cannot accomplish their goals and missions alone. A leader must develop and mold people into effective teams and support their efforts and goals. Teamwork is successful when team members are willing to put the organizational goals before their own interests.

5. Honor

Honor is a philosophy – a set of behaviors you choose. This behavior identifies you as a "person of honor." Honor is also defined as a "nobility of mind." At West Point, honor is defined as no lying, cheating, or stealing, or tolerating people who do.

6. Commitment

Devotion to your duty. Plato said: "Man was not born for himself alone, but for his country." Commitment is an essential trait in any leader.

7. Loyalty

Three-way trait: being faithful to your employees, your organization, and your peers. You can't expect loyalty from your followers if you're not loyal to them.

8. Energy

Mental and physical endurance. Enthusiasm and drive to get things done. Stamina to keep working until the job is done.

9. Selflessness

Leaders don't worry about getting credit for a

success. They place the welfare of their people and the accomplishment of the organization's mission over personal gains. The ability and willingness to put the needs and requirement of your people and organization above your own personal goals.

10. Decisiveness
The ability to make decisions quickly and implement them is a clear, forceful manner. This is a must, under pressure situations. It's not too difficult to lead during easy times, but it's much more difficult to lead during times of stress.

All these traits are important, but the most important ones are character and integrity. Without these traits, a leader will eventually be exposed, and lose the respect of his or her followers and their willingness to follow.

Chapter Four

The Importance of Listening

"Formula for handling people:
1) Listen to the other person's story;
2) Listen to the other person's full story;
3) Listen to the other person's full story first."
General George C. Marshall

Being a good listener is an essential skill for a good leader. When I was a kid, my father used to constantly tell me that people never learn when they're talking, only when they're listening. This advice has been valuable for me throughout my academic, military, and corporate life. All leaders should keep this advice in mind and, through good listening skills, constantly learn more about the people they lead.

Solicited Vs. Unsolicited Advice
A good leader listens to unsolicited advice. It's critical for a leader to be responsive and available to listen to his or her workers. However, in my experience, unsolicited advice isn't necessarily very helpful. Many times, a person offering unsolicited advice has a hidden agenda, offering advice that's best for that person, but not necessarily in the best interest of the organization.

"The desk is a dangerous place from
which to watch the world."
John LeCarré

Solicited advice offers a higher quality of information, and several advantages. First, it gets you out of your office and takes you to your employees' work locations. You can then focus on the areas that are critical to your operation and ask your employees for their feedback and advice.

Always listen to all your people, and accept their unsolicited advice. However, remember the most valuable advice is most likely to be the advice you solicit.

Second, it honors the person you ask, who'll feel pleased that the boss is actually seeking his or her opinion, which raises morale. The third advantage is that the person you ask will be more likely to give an unbiased opinion, rather than one laced with self-interest. Therefore, always listen to all your people, and accept their unsolicited advice. However, remember the most valuable advice is most likely to be the advice you solicit.

Open Communications

"Followers 'have a say' in what they
are being led to. A leader who neglects
that fact soon finds him (her) self
without followers."
Garry Wills

Besides just listening, every leader should also engage in open communications. When I reported to my first organization, the 101st Airborne Division, in the 1960s, I was a young second lieutenant, fresh from West Point. This was a very tough outfit. All of us in my company, even the officers, were afraid of our senior enlisted man, First Sergeant Cardenas. He was a very rough, tough soldier with many years of experience.   However, I decided to try and take advantage of his experience.

Although I outranked him, I knew I could learn valuable leadership lessons from him. Instead of avoiding him like everyone else, I approached him and asked him to join me for a cup of coffee. I admitted to him that as a new lieutenant I recognized my inexperience.

I asked him if he'd give me his advice and guidance from time to time as I encountered problems I was unsure how to handle. He said he wasn't in the habit of helping lieutenants, but because I was the first one to ever actually ask for his advice, he'd give me a hand whenever I needed it.

Front that point on, I asked his advice whenever I was unsure about what to do in certain difficult situations. With the benefits of his expert advice, I was able to overcome the learning curve much easier than most beginning officers. Even though I was in a higher position in the organization and better educated, he was my teacher.

Many times, the most knowledgeable people in an organization aren't the highest ranking or best educated ones. It's important that you listen to people within your organization, regardless of their rank or position. They'll oftentimes surprise you with their knowledge and insights. Once you've opened the lines of communication, make sure they stay open, so you never stop learning.

Important Lessons from Unexpected Sources

Great information often comes from unexpected sources, such as chance meetings, or coincidences. I was born and raised in Kosciusko, Mississippi during the late fifties and early sixties in a totally segregated society, when black people went to separate schools, separate restaurants, and even drank from separate drinking fountains. Although I had planned on attending the University of Mississippi after high school, I changed my plans after being accepted to West Point.

> **Once you've opened the lines of communication, make sure they stay open, so you never stop learning.**

Fortunately, during my four years at West Point, I was exposed to a much wider range of ideas than I had experienced in central Mississippi, especially concerning the evils of segregation. However, when my company, in the 101st Airborne Division, was suddenly called in to control the infamous riots at the University of Mississippi campus, I learned some valuable lessons from a totally unexpected source.

The rioting started when the first black man,

James Meredith, attempted to enter the then segregated university. The white students started burning cars and buildings on campus, raiding campus offices, attacking black people, and destroying any property they could find. Being a part of the military force that engaged the rioters was a strange experience for me, because the students were all about my age and from the same segregated Mississippi background. Although my loyalty was totally to the United States Army, I felt very uneasy about the situation.

Even after the initial riots, people still continued to try to stop Meredith from attending classes. They harassed him on his way to and from class, and therefore, he had to be constantly escorted by federal marshals during the day. At night, my company from the 101st Airborne guarded him in his dorm. I was the officer in charge of his guard detail. My men were stationed all over the building, on every floor, and for a few days my duty station was a chair right outside his dorm door. Essentially, I was the last line of his defense. Several times during this period, he invited me to his room, where we'd have long conversations.

During these talks, I learned some very important lessons from an unexpected source. He explained to me in great detail how it felt to be on the black side of a segregated society. I had never really thought about a segregated society from a black man's point of view. After listening to him tell of his many experiences growing up, I learned a great deal about the evils of segregation and about seeing situations from different perspectives.

It turned out that Meredith was also from my home town of Kosciusko, Mississippi. By coincidence, we had lived in the same small town, at the same time, but in a completely different and separate segregated community. Of course, we never knew each other, because we never had the opportunity to be in the same high school, or in the same restaurant, or at the same drinking fountain. However, our paths magically crossed at a very pivotal time in history. This experience taught me that a person can learn great lessons from very unexpected sources – if one is open to learning from these sources.

> **One caution to keep in mind as you listen to people: watch what they do, as well as listen to what they say.**

As a side note, the town of Kosciusko was named after a Polish general, who came here during the American Revolution to help us defeat the British. Incidentally, another famous person, Oprah Winfrey, is originally from Kosciusko. Although it's a small rural town, it has played a significant role in our history.

A Caution about Listening

One caution to keep in mind as you listen to people: watch what they do, as well as listen to what they say. I've found that in the military, when new leaders take charge of an organization, they meet with everyone to explain their policies and how they intend to run the organization. These new commanders undoubtedly believed in their stated policies and standards.

However, I've learned that a leader's or manager's true policies and standards are determined by the decisions they make and the actions they take during critical times, and not by what they say.

This concept carries over into the corporate world. Many times, I've heard corporate leaders — even CEOs — talk about the values and goals of their organizations. However, often their subsequent decisions are inconsistent with their stated policies. Therefore, listen to what people have to say, but carefully observe their behavior and decision making to determine their real policies, standards and goals.

CHAPTER FIVE

CHOOSING THE BEST

"When building a team,
I always search for people who love to win.
If I can't find any of those,
I look for people who hate to lose."
H. Ross Perot

The most important asset a company has is its people. As discussed in Chapter 1, the difference between companies is usually the quality of their people and their leadership, and not the quality of their products and services.

Hire the Best People with the Best Character

"The best executive is the one who has
sense enough to pick good men to do
what he wants done, and self-restraint to
keep from meddling with them while they do it."
Theodore Roosevelt

Usually in the corporate world, a person with ten years' experience will be hired instead of a person with five years' experience, regardless of which one is a better person. In my opinion, in the vast majority of cases, you should hire the best person, rather than the most technically qualified or most experienced one.

Of course, the person you hire must meet the minimum qualifications for the position. Employers must learn to look beyond experience, and focus more on character, motivation, and work ethic. You can always teach a job to someone with the proper qualifications, but you can't teach integrity, drive, loyalty, dedication, punctuality, and the desire to put forth extra effort to get things accomplished. Most people can learn a set of job skills, but these personal characteristics either come with a person or they don't, regardless of that person's employment history.

> **You can always teach a job to someone with the proper qualifications, but you can't teach integrity, drive, loyalty, dedication, punctuality, and the desire to put forth extra effort to get things accomplished.**

"What characteristics do I look for in hiring someone? That's one of the questions I ask in interviewing, I want to know what kind of people they would hire."
Jeff Bezos, CEO, Amazon.com, Inc.

When I was the country Operations Director for Motorola in Prague in the Czech Republic, I interviewed a German engineer flown in from Motorola Germany. He had the experience and qualifications I needed to fill a particular position. However, in the interview all he talked about was what he wouldn't do. He wouldn't work weekends, and only under certain conditions would he put in extra hours. I ended the interview abruptly and sent him back to Germany on the next plane. Although he had all the needed qualifications, he lacked the work ethic and attitude to be successful in the organization.

Another example of the importance of hiring people with great character comes from history. In December 1914, an expedition of 28 men led by Sir Ernest Shackleton sailed from South Georgia Island in the South Atlantic aboard the ship "Endurance." Their mission was to land on Antarctica and become the first expedition to cross that continent. However, the Shackleton expedition never even set foot on Antarctica. Yet the courage and leadership these 28 men displayed during the next two years is one of the greatest adventure stories ever told.

Before they reached Antarctica, their ship became trapped in the ice in the Waddell Sea. For over two years, these men suffered a series of catastrophic events that should have resulted in their deaths many times. After six months of being trapped in the ice, their ship was crushed by floating ice, forcing them into lifeboats in which they drifted for the next six months.

After many more setbacks, they finally made their way to safety. Amazingly, after two years under the harshest conditions imaginable, all 28 men survived. Shackleton was obviously a great leader who was able to lead a dangerous exploration through near-disaster without fatality or mutiny.

However, his success was due in great measure to his knack for picking the right men for the rigors of this very challenging expedition. His memoirs indicated that he made a great effort to select crew members with strong characters – not just technical competence.

Many of the crew members later wrote in their memoirs that they were very surprised at the questions Shackleton asked during their interviews. He didn't ask anyone a single question about their technical qualifications. Instead, he asked about their hobbies, activities, families, their outlook on life, and their character traits. He wanted to know how well they performed under pressure, about their loyalty, their ability to work as a team, and their mental toughness – not about their exploration experiences or technical competence.

The selection and development of leaders is one of the most important tasks for senior leaders. Selecting and developing junior leaders ensures the future of the organization.

The key point is that you should hire people more for their character than for their years of experience or technical qualifications.

Select the Best Leaders

Not only do senior leaders need to choose the best followers, they must also select the best leaders to fill the leadership positions in their organization. The selection and development of leaders is one of the most important tasks for senior leaders. Selecting and developing junior leaders ensures the future of the organization. In the military, many senior officers are known as leaders who have the ability to develop other leaders. These senior officers are held in very high regard. I've seldom seen a similar pattern in the corporate world.

In fact, I've seen cases where senior corporate leaders don't want to develop junior leaders, because they fear the possible competition. This is clearly a very short-sighted view. Organizations should have specific programs that encourage and even reward leaders who develop other leaders.

Four or five months before the start of Desert Storm, I was serving my last year of a three-year tour as a Brigadier General at the United States Embassy in Korea. Because I had a year left there, I expected to miss Desert Storm. Much to my surprise, I got a call from the Pentagon requesting that I leave Korea early and take command of the XVIIIth Airborne Corps Artillery in Saudi Arabia.

The officer from the Pentagon said the Army had decided to put its most qualified leaders and proven combat commanders in charge of the Desert Storm combat units, which involved responsibility for thousands of our soldiers in a combat zone as they prepared to attack Iraq.

Later, after I decided to retire from the military, I sent my résumé to several corporations. Surprisingly, I was called to the Motorola headquarters in Chicago from Fort Bragg, North Carolina to interview for a position as the director of project management for a billion dollar cellular telephone project.

I had no Signal Corps or cellular experience. In the interview, I said I was honored that Motorola would consider me for this position, but that I'd never even owned a cellular phone. I though I'd be on the next plane out of Chicago. However, they said they could teach me the technical aspects of the cellular phone business.

> **The leaders (the senior executives, the presidents, the CEOs, etc.) in any organization should play an active role in the leadership selection process and be the decision makers.**

They were interested in me because of my leadership qualifications. Motorola, at that time and in that sub-organization, chose people for leadership positions based on experience and ability, and not on achievements and longevity.

Cautions

Whose responsibility is it to identify and hire leaders? Many corporations leave much of the responsibility to the Human Resources Department. However, it's the responsibility of senior leaders to pick junior leaders. I once had a commander in the military named Colonel Max Thurman, who said: "Personnel decisions, especially picking people for leadership positions, are too important to leave to the Human Resources People." The leaders (the senior executives, the presidents, the CEOs, etc.) in any organization should play an active role in the leadership selection process and be the decision makers.

As previously mentioned in Chapter 1, once the leaders are chosen, their training must be extensive and often. Usually, in the corporate world, a new leader is sent to a two- or three-week leadership seminar and then is 'anointed" as a leader. However, a two-week training course alone won't cut it. All leaders, including the highest senior executives, must continue to receive additional leadership training several times a year, in order to maximize their leadership potential and effectiveness.

An additional note: leadership training in the Army is almost always given by a person who has actually been a successful leader in the real world. This isn't always true in the corporate world. Having an academic knowledge of leadership is valuable, but this knowledge can't replace real leadership experience under difficult conditions.

Final Note

The success of your organization will be more a function of the quality of your employees and leaders than the quality of your products and services. Leaders must always be involved in all personnel decisions and training – do not delegate this critical responsibility.

CHAPTER 6

POWER AND EGO

"Oh, it is excellent to have a giant's strength,
But it is tyrannous to use it like a giant."
William Shakespeare

Power

Abraham Lincoln once said: "Nearly all men can stand adversity, but if you want to test a man's character give him power." Power is good, as long as it's used for the good of the organization, and not for personal gain or to intimidate others. We want our leaders to have power, in order to get things done, overcome inertia, surmount obstacles, and complete the mission, whether it's a corporate or military mission. Therefore, power used correctly is appropriate and necessary for a leader.

I've never seen any leader who used power for his or her own gain be successful in the long term.

We've all seen examples of people using power for their own personal gain. Fortunately, in well-led organizations, this is almost always eventually recognized by more senior people and dealt with appropriately. Unfortunately, some leaders get away with this behavior for some time. However, I've never seen any leader who used power for his or her own gain be successful in the long term. In the vast majority of cases, these people quickly lose the respect of their workers, peers, and bosses.

> ***"You don't lead by hitting people over the head
> —that's assault, not leadership."***
> ***Dwight D. Eisenhower***

Others use power to "rule by fear" and intimidate people. Some people believe that, during times of great pressure, the "rule by fear" technique can be somewhat effective for the short term. For example, it might be used in a combat situation, when there's no time to get the opinions and recommendations of others, and where instant and unquestioned obedience is necessary for survival. In the corporate world, it could be used just before a big event, such as a merger or major inspection, where there's little or no time for normal leadership techniques.

I've unfortunately encountered "rule by fear" leaders a few times in my career. In Vietnam, during one of my tours, I was a captain in the operations section of the 1st Infantry Division. The Division G3 (Operations Officer) absolutely ruled by fear and intimidation. He was effective due to the dire combat situation, but after Vietnam he was eventually exposed as a poor leader, and didn't have a long and successful career. His people didn't respect him, and made every effort to get transferred to other organizations.

I don't believe that "fear and intimidation leadership techniques" are ever appropriate or effective.

"He who has power should use it lightly."
Seneca

I've seen strong leaders accomplish great things under the most intense leadership conditions – combat – without resorting to fear techniques. People who use "rule by fear" aren't real leaders, but simply bullies. They don't respect their followers and their followers don't respect them. These types of "leaders" don't develop independent thinking leaders, which is very bad for the future of any organization.

> **People who use "rule by fear" aren't real leaders, but simply bullies. They don't respect their followers and their followers don't respect them.**

Unfortunately, many of these "rule by fear" types are successful in the short term because they drive results. However, when the crisis is passed and the organization returns to a normal operational tempo, they're eventually recognized as poor leaders and are unsuccessful in the long term.

In many cases, it's the lack of power that corrupts people more than power does. In the military, in the government, and probably in most corporations, there's a phenomenon called bureaucracy, which can absolutely stifle operational efficiency. Bureaucracy is really the misuse of power, by people who don't have much power.

These people set up rules, regulations, procedures, and forms, designed to increase their power and control in the organization. Each of these rules

In many cases, it's the lack of power that corrupts people more than power does.

and regulations might seem reasonable when viewed alone. However, add many of them together and you have bureaucracy.

Key Point: One very important responsibility of every leader is to make sure employees are not inappropriately using their limited power to create bureaucracies.

Ego

"The well-run group is not a battlefield of egos."
Lao-tzu

Ego is the "twin" of power, and I think it sometimes gets a bad name. I've heard some leaders say there'll be no egos allowed in their organization. This is unrealistic. Egos are a natural emotion for humans and cannot be successfully outlawed. If you don't have a healthy ego before you make general in the Army, or vice president, general manager or CEO in the corporate world, you'll definitely get one after the promotion.

A healthy ego is necessary for a leader and works to his or her advantage if it's not overdone. A healthy ego and confidence go hand-in-hand. The only problem with an ego is that you must keep it under control. If your ego gets too big, you'll become overbearing to your workers and coworkers.

The trick is to keep your ego under control. To do that, leaders must realize they have an ego, and be open to people "helping them" keep it under control. Of course, our spouses are expert at keeping our egos in line. They simply say, "Mr. Senior Vice President, or Mr. General Manager, or Mr. General Officer, take out the garbage." Listen to your spouses – they'll help you with your ego – I guarantee it!

I've had my ego expertly deflated several times in the Army. Each year, several senior generals come to the Pentagon to serve on a selection board that chooses approximately forty new brigadier generals from a list of several thousand outstanding and very qualified colonels. To select only forty is extremely difficult.

> **A healthy ego is necessary for a leader and works to his or her advantage if it's not overdone. A healthy ego and confidence go hand-in-hand.**

When one's name is announced as among the "chosen few," there's a great feeling of pride, followed closely by a great increase in ego. Shortly after being selected, each person attends a two-week course often referred to as the "General Officer Charm School Course." This course teaches what's expected of general officers, and provides a wealth of advice and practical information.

I remember all forty of us together for the first time – our egos barely fit into the big room. The Chief of Staff of the Army congratulated us in a rather gruff way, and then took a copy of our promotion list and tore it up! He told us that if he really did reject the list, he could tell the selection board to give him forty different names and those forty officers would be just as good, if not better, than we were. He added that he could reject that list and ask for a third one, which would be of equal quality. The sounds of egos being deflated in the room was deafening!

In that same meeting, he gave us the best advice I ever had — that I didn't follow. He told us that just because we were being promoted to brigadier generals didn't mean we'd be deprived of any of the constitutional rights enjoyed by every other American citizen. He noted that one of those rights was to keep our mouths shut, and that we should exercise that right as often as possible!

Unfortunately for me, I didn't always heed his advice. In my personal, military, and corporate life, I've often gotten into trouble when I failed to exercise my constitutional right to keep my mouth shut. I'd wager that some readers have had the same problem from time to time.

I received another ego adjustment as a brigadier general in combat in Iraq during Desert Storm. As the Commanding General of the XVIIIth Airborne Corps Artillery, I traveled in a Humvee with my driver, bodyguards and a senior sergeant. For those who haven't been in the military, each organization in the Army has an officer commander and a senior sergeant, who's the commander's "right hand man." The senior sergeant in the organization has a rank of First Sergeant, or Command Sergeant Major, depending on the size of the organization.

The commander and the sergeant stay close together day and night, so they can quickly assess any new situation or combat emergency and take the proper actions and give the correct orders to the organization. When there's an opportunity to get a little sleep, the commander and sergeant share the same tent.

On the second night in Iraq, the battle had temporarily decreased in intensity and we realized we could get about two or three hours of sleep. I thought I'd take this opportunity to show all the enlisted people what a good officer I was by doing some work and helping erect the tent. I said: "Sergeant Major, how long will it take us to put up the tent?" With great respect, he replied: "Sir, ten minutes if I do it, twenty minutes if you help."

My ego was immediately deflated. I thought about it for a few seconds and said, "Sergeant Major, I think I have some officer business to attend to." He proceeded to put the tent up in ten minutes, without any "help" from me.

I had a third ego-deflating situation while I was the Chief of Staff (Colonel) of the 82nd Airborne Division, stationed at Fort Bragg, North Carolina. A brigade (about 2000 paratroopers) from the division, using in-flight refueling, flew directly from Fort Bragg and parachuted into Egypt for a joint operation with Egyptian paratrooper forces. I parachuted with the brigade before dawn on a hot windy day.

This operation took place at a time when Egypt and Israel were bitter enemies and had recently fought a war. I participated in the ground phase of the operation for a few days, but had to return to the U.S. before the operation was over. I traveled to the Cairo airport with a ticket for a commercial flight back home. Due to the sensitive military situation, I wore civilian clothes, which were required when traveling separately from your military unit.

Heavily armed Egyptian soldiers ran the airport. When I got to the checkout counter, I showed the Egyptian sergeant my U.S. passport. He carefully looked at it and asked why I didn't have the required stamp, showing I had entered Egypt legally. I started explaining that I parachuted into Egypt as part of a joint U.S.-Egypt military operation.

When he heard the words "parachuted into Egypt," he jumped up and shouted "You are an Israeli spy." I said, "No, no, I'm not an Israeli spy, I'm an American military officer and a part of a joint operation with your Army – and I have an American passport."

The Egyptian sergeant was not a good listener. He got very excited and said that many Israeli spies have American passports, and that my story was clearly a cover story. I was immediately arrested and dragged off, by two burly soldiers with bad attitudes, to a little jail cell in the airport, all the while hoping they'd check out my story before they started the beatings.

Fortunately, my story was verified by an Egyptian officer about four hours after I was jailed, and before the "interrogation" started. I missed my flight, but I was happy to be in one piece. I entered the situation as a "big shot" senior U.S. military officer with a big ego, but I was quickly reduced to being a victim who feared for my life and safety. I tell my Jewish friends I should be named an honorary Israeli, because I'd been arrested and jailed for being an Israeli spy. Not many Southern Baptist boys from Mississippi have had that experience.

Another time when my ego was deflated was in a combat situation on the little island of Grenada. Grenada is a beautiful tropical island off the coast of South America, and is a favorite stop for many cruise ships. In the early 80s, Grenada was being used by Fidel Castro as a military supply base to support communist insurgencies in Central and South America.

There were many large warehouses of military equipment on the island, containing ammunition, military clothing, and thousands of AK 47 assault rifles. Approximately a thousand Cuban soldiers, led by a Cuban colonel, were operating the supply base.

Additionally, there was a large medical school on the island with many American students. It was one of several Caribbean medical schools at that time that catered to American students who failed to gain entrance to U.S. medical schools. The elected governor of Grenada was overthrown and a new pro-Cuba communist or socialist governor took power.

The U.S. was concerned about the safety of the American students who were being threatened by the Grenadian military. There was also great concern about what Castro was going to do with all the military supplies on the island. Based on these concerns, the U.S. decided to invade Grenada to save the students, confiscate the military supplies, and rid the island of the communist governor.

The invasion consisted of the U.S. Marines attacking the northern part of the island and the Army paratroopers from the Army Rangers and 82nd Airborne Division making a parachute and air-land assault on south side of the island. The parachute assault and the air-land operation were conducted on the Grenada Airport just before dawn, to achieve surprise and to minimize the chances of getting paratroopers shot while descending in their parachutes.

After a parachute operation, there's always a period of time where the paratroopers from various tactical units get reoriented and assemble at their own individual unit rendezvous points on the drop zone before attacking their objectives. This period of "reorganization and consolidation" can be a very confusing time.

In this case, there was a great deal of enemy fire coming from anti-aircraft guns located on the hills surrounding the airport. Luckily, these guns did no damage, because our jump altitude was under their lowest trajectory. This was pure luck because we didn't know of the existence of these potentially devastating weapons. There was also enemy fire coming from a ground attack by the Grenadian and Cuban soldiers from the south end of the airport runway.

A little background: officers normally are armed with pistols rather than rifles. However, I learned in Vietnam that it's very important that an officer carry a rifle in addition to the pistol. Enemy snipers are trying to identify officers as targets by looking for people without rifles. In addition, in a firefight, a rifle has more firepower, accuracy, and range than a pistol.

In the initial confusion, I saw a ranger about 15 yards away on one knee, firing at the enemy on the end of the runway. I knew he was a ranger by the shape of his steel helmet and the markings on it. At that time, I was a full colonel. Normally, a low-ranking soldier has little opportunity to talk to a colonel and, when it does happen, it's usually a major event for the soldier.

In the still dark early morning, illuminated only by incoming and outgoing tracer bullets I knelt down beside that young ranger and, in my best colonel's voice said, "Ranger, where are the front lines?" Without hesitation, and while continuing to fire, he said, "You're standing on them, you dumb son of a bitch."

Now, low-ranking soldiers simply don't talk to colonels that way. My ego was immediately deflated, and I knelt in stunned silence trying to determine what to say in response. He continued to fire and, after a few seconds, he said, "Are you going to fire your rifle or what?" Clearly, he wanted some help in defeating the enemy attack.

I later met the soldier down at his ranger unit. By then, he had learned who I was and was afraid a court martial might be in his future. However, I eased his mind and told him I realized he thought I was another enlisted soldier because of my rifle. We had a good laugh and a cup of coffee – all was forgiven.

The lesson is that you need to be prepared to have your ego deflated at your workplace and allow that to happen without getting too upset.

One caution on the subject of ego; If one of your leaders is unable to control his or her ego, that person must be replaced in the short term, regardless of performance, because the long-term damage to the organization outweighs any positive performance considerations.

CHAPTER 7

BEING A GOOD FOLLOWER

"Different situations call for different leaders.
A leader is not a leader in every situation."
Kenneth A. Wells
Guide to Good Leadership

In every organization, there are many people in leadership positions at several different levels. Clearly, every leader can't be the prime leader in every situation. The military strongly emphasizes the need for a leader to be a good follower as the situation dictates. In the corporate world, this concept is recognized but isn't strongly emphasized. Based on my experience, this is one of the main differences between the corporate world and the military world.

When legal and legitimate decisions are made by a higher authority or more senior leaders, the other leaders in the organization must, in effect, become followers and fully support that decision.

Supporting Decisions

When legal and legitimate decisions are made by a higher authority or more senior leaders, the other leaders in the organization must, in effect, become followers and fully support that decision. In the Army, there's very, very open communication. Before a final decision is made on any issue, officers at every level are encouraged to give their opinions and strongly state their recommendations in a strong and decisive way.

However, once the decision is made by the appropriate leader, every person is expected to support it one hundred percent. In fact, the people who made recommendations different from the final decision are expected, more so than anybody else, to support that decision with all their heart and soul.

Based on my experience in the corporate world, the tradition of fully open communications and totally supporting decisions isn't as prevalent as in the military. This was one of my first and biggest surprises in the corporate world, where I found that many executives were very careful to avoid making any recommendations they thought might be contrary to the views of their boss. Many of them waited until they sensed what the boss thought on an issue, and then threw their support in that direction. One executive called this "voting after the results are in."

This lack of open communication results in alternative and possibly superior recommendations never being revealed or discussed. I also found that after important decisions were made, they weren't always fully supported by all the executives. In many cases, executives who had made different recommendations often would support the decision on the surface – but not with all their heart and soul. Their support would be slightly off – one or two degrees.

Many clearly had their own agendas, often hoping the adopted decision will be proven wrong, thus justifying their own original recommendations.

Due to the differences between the military and corporate worlds in the areas of open communication and fully supporting decisions, I often pondered the question: Are military officers more honest and straightforward than their corporate counterparts?

At one time, I believed that to be the case, but I now realize it's the result of differences in the two cultures.

In the corporate world, executives are compensated with bonuses, pay raises, and stock options based on short-term results – monthly, quarterly and annual reports. Therefore, the corporate culture tends to make people not want to openly make risky recommendations or be too closely connected to a decision that might fail.

In the military, the pay for a particular rank and time in the military is fixed. Pay raises are set by Congress; there are no stock options and no short-term financial reports. As a result, military officers tend to think more long-term than their corporate counterparts, because they have no short-term monetary incentives.

In the corporate world promotions are often determined by one person – the next higher boss. In the military, officer promotions are based on fixed time in grades (set minimum number of years at a given rank). Promotions are determined by selection boards comprised of 10-20 officers based on the annual OERs (Officer Efficiency Reports) from many years of service. Therefore, executives in the corporate world must be very careful that they stay on the "right side" of their bosses.

From Leader to Follower

My career has been full of times when the situation caused me to become a follower. As a major, I returned to West Point as an Assistant Professor of Mathematics. I had just completed a combat tour in Vietnam, where I'd been a combat leader with almost absolute authority. Unlike a normal military unit, there are many, many high ranking officers stationed in the Tactical and Academic Departments at West Point. Instead of being one of the highest ranking officers, I was now one of the lowest ranking officers in the organization and immediately had to adjust to being a follower rather than a senior leader.

Teaching at West Point was a great tour, but it did require an adjustment from being a VIP to being a "worker bee." A similar situation occurs when an officer is assigned to the rank-heavy Pentagon.

After my retirement from the Army, I accepted a position with Motorola in Chicago. After two years there, I was sent to Japan to be Motorola's Director of Engineering and Operations. I lived with my family near Osaka on a man-made island just off the coast of Kobe, Japan, on the 26th floor of an apartment building. Most of the people on the island were high ranking executives from several large American companies. We were all senior leaders in our companies.

One morning at about six as I was shaving, Kobe was hit with one of the most powerful earthquakes recorded in the world in many, many years. The earthquake, with the resulting fires and collapsing buildings, killed thousands of people and destroyed tens of thousands of buildings in a ten-minute period. Fortunately, my apartment building didn't collapse, but was badly damaged as it swayed more than 25 feet back and forth during the 30-second earthquake. I was a retired general with a great deal of combat experience but it did me little good – I immediately became a victim to this powerful act of Mother Nature.

The bridges to the mainland were totally destroyed, isolating the people on the island from the outside world. Because this was a manmade island, there was a real danger that it would sink and disappear into the ocean. All these senior leaders were now helpless followers. Our survival depended on cooperating with all the other people on the island.

There was an elementary school and high school on the island that was built to withstand earthquakes, so the entire population of the island (about 500 people) went to the school to live until we were rescued. We slept in the halls, and consolidated all our available food. Although I had extensive leadership experience, I immediately saw the need to be a member of the group of executives and be a follower when required.

Several of us accepted limited leadership positions – such as being in charge of gathering food or supervising the digging of ditches for use as bathrooms – but we were followers in other areas. After about a week, we were rescued from the island by a passenger boat that was rented by a Proctor & Gamble executive who was sent from the U.S. to rescue us "refugees" on the island. In this very unusual situation, all the senior executives on the island had to immediately learn to be good followers and be productive members of the group.

On the last day of combat in Desert Storm in Iraq, I had to again revert from being a leader to a follower in a crisis situation. I was leading more than ten thousand artillery and rocket soldiers in the attack against the Iraqi elite Republican Guard. The coalition forces had successfully liberated Kuwait and had trapped the entire Iraqi force near Basra, Iraq in an area bounded by the Euphrates River on the north and the Persian Gulf on the east.

The U.S. XVIIIth Airborne Corps, of which I was a part, blocked any escape from the west and the U.S. VIIth Corps blocked the Iraqi force from the south. The war was over for all practical purposes. After months of preparation in the hot Saudi Arabian desert and a 100-hour war, we had the enemy trapped and beaten. Our orders were to attack at dawn and destroy or capture the Iraqi forces. Having been in this area of the world for many months, we were very much in a war-fighting mood.

However, because the enemy was helpless and trying to escape rather than fight, a decision was made due to humanitarian reasons to cancel the final attack and accept the surrender of the Iraqi army. We received new orders to disarm the Iraqi forces and let the soldiers cross the Euphrates River to the north and go home.

After starting the process, we were then told to let the Republican Guard keep their individual and heavy weapons and return to Baghdad. I immediately thought this order must have been transmitted incorrectly. Surely we weren't going to let the best Iraqi Divisions return to Baghdad with their full complement of weapons and ammunition.

All the officers in my organization and many of the American generals were very, very surprised at this order. We were concerned that if we let the Republican Guards go with their weapons, they'd simply go back to Baghdad and protect Saddam Hussein. One of the U.S. objectives in the war was the removal of Saddam Hussein by an uprising of the Iraqi Kurdish and Shia Muslims who had been persecuted by Saddam. If we released the Republican Guard, any chance of an uprising would be greatly reduced.

This was a time in my career where I needed to be a follower and hope the officials who issued this very controversial order were doing the right thing. We followed the orders and released the Republican Guard. Unfortunately, our fears were well-founded. The Republican Guard returned to Baghdad, protected Saddam and killed

I'm convinced we're back in Iraq today because of this unfortunate order which prevented us from finishing the job.

hundreds if not thousands of the Kurds and Shias who were plotting his overthrow. I'm convinced we're back in Iraq today because of this unfortunate order which prevented us from finishing the job.

Every good leader must be prepared to be a good follower. The key is to have the "sixth sense" to know when to revert from leader to follower. That moment will be obvious most of the time. People will be reluctant to follow you if you're unable to revert to being a follower when appropriate. As the late Sam Rayburn, a famous Speaker of the U.S. House of Representatives, once said:

> *"You cannot be a leader and ask others to follow you unless you know how to follow, too."*

CHAPTER 8

LEADING BY EXAMPLE

*"The quality of a leader is reflected
in the standards they set for themselves."*
Ray Kroc, McDonald's Founder

All leadership principles are important. However, this leadership principle – lead by example – was the most important one to me personally during my 32-year military career. It was the basis of my personal leadership style. In my view, all real leaders lead by example – no exceptions.

Leading by example means the leader sets the standards for the people in an organization on how to behave and perform their duties and responsibilities by his or her actions and attitudes. Part of leading by example is obeying the rules. Every organization has a set of rules, regulations, travel standards, standards of personal conduct, etc. required by the organization. However, leaders are often tempted to make exceptions for themselves, because it saves time, or is more convenient, or they're in a big hurry.

Some poor leaders believe the rules are made for others but don't apply to them. However, leading by example is much more than just obeying your own organizational rules. Leadership is an art rather than a science. A leader who truly leads by example takes charge and creates an atmosphere that inspires the people in the organization. The "leads by example" leader operates well above the minimum standards and sets the example in all areas by his or her daily conduct, sense of responsibility, integrity, fairness, and attitude.

"When put in charge, take charge."
Major General Max Thurman

People Are Watching

All leaders must realize someone is the organization is observing everything they do and say all of the time. Leader cannot fool their employees for very long. If you're not leading by example, your people throughout the organization will know. At that time, your status as a leader, your credibility, and your ability to effectively lead the organization will be greatly reduced.

Leadership is an art rather than a science. A leader who truly leads by example creates an atmosphere that inspires the people in the organization.

The small advantages and time savings you might gain from not complying with the standards of the organization are clearly not worth the great price you pay with your loss of credibility as a leader. Leading by example is sometimes hard and takes a great deal of effort. However, if your people recognize that you lead by example, the benefits to you as a leader and to your organization will be enormous.

Leading by example can be very important even when you're not in a regular leadership position in an organization. One of my favorite tours in the Army was as an Assistant Professor of Mathematics at the United States Military Academy at West Point, NY. This academic position was not a traditional leadership position – yet setting the example was still very important.

The mathematics instructors were expected not only to be academic instructors but to set a strong military example for the young plebes (freshmen) by their military bearing, attitude, and professionalism. Leaders should always lead by example, even when they're not in a leadership position, so they'll affect people in a positive manner.

> **Leading by example is sometimes hard and takes a great deal of effort. However, if your people recognize that you lead by example, the benefits to you as a leader and to your organization will be enormous.**

Leading by Example Under Fire

> *"A leader leads by example*
> *whether he intends to or not."*
> **Unknown**

Leading by example always requires effort, dedication, and determination. However, leading by example during the good times when business is booming or the work situation is ideal isn't too difficult. The test of a true leader is how that leader performs during the hard times or adverse situations – leading under fire.

When I was a 17-year-old Plebe (freshman) at West Point, I had a boxing instructor who was a legend – "Punchy" Creighton. Punchy really pushed the cadet boxers to fight fiercely, never give up, and bleed a little. He would tell us over and over: "It's not if you get knocked down, it's how you get up."

The test of a true leader is how that leader performs during the hard times or adverse situations – leading under fire.

Every person will have some great adversity in life – that's a given. You will get knocked down from time to time. The important thing is getting up and reacting positively to that adversity. Leaders will also encounter adverse conditions. True leaders will "rise to the occasion," and perform at their best under these conditions.

Some of the most important lessons in life are learned from unexpected sources. I learned leading by example under adverse conditions from an enemy soldier – a North Vietnamese captain during the Vietnam War. I was an artillery battery commander with the U.S. 1st Infantry Division operating in the Michelin Rubber plantation north of Saigon, near the Cambodian border.

An artillery battery has six 105MM howitzers and about 100 men. During this period, artillery batteries were placed in "night defensive positions," sometimes called fire bases, located deep in the jungles in enemy controlled territory. The purpose of these fire bases was to put the artillery units in position or in range to provide critical artillery support to the infantry battalions making air mobile (helicopter) assaults against enemy positions. All the artillerymen realized we were deep in enemy territory and in an extremely vulnerable and dangerous situation.

On this occasion, we were co-located with an infantry company of about 200 men, so there was a total of 300 U.S. soldiers in fire base danger near Loch Ninh, Vietnam. At about 10 p.m., we were attacked by a North Vietnamese regiment of about 1,200 well-trained and motivated enemy soldiers. They continued to attack our positions with frontal assaults throughout the night. On two occasions, they penetrated our defensive lines and had to be repelled by hand-to-hand fighting.

Throughout the long night, we could hear the North Vietnamese officers shouting encouragement to their men, blowing their whistles, and trying to lead them to victory and overrun the fire base. Finally, at dawn, the North Vietnamese broke off the attack and crossed over into Cambodia. They realized we'd be getting additional air support and it would be too dangerous for them to continue the attack in daylight.

After the attack, we got out of our bunkers to see if any enemy soldiers needed medical attention, get any intelligence information from the bodies of the dead North Vietnamese soldiers, and then bury them. The enemy had managed to take their wounded soldiers with them, but there were more than 200 North Vietnamese bodies that had to be buried immediately, due to the hot and humid climate.

Most of their dead were within 10-40 feet of our defensive bunkers. About 30 feet from my bunker was a dead North Vietnamese captain in his bright blue uniform, leaning against a rubber tree. He still had his pistol in his hand and his whistle in his mouth. I noticed in amazement that his leg had been blown off from his knee down. He had taken his belt from his trousers and tied a tourniquet around his stump.

Based on the blood trail leading up to the rubber tree, his leg had been blown off some distance back. He had obviously tied the tourniquet around his stump and dragged himself along the ground toward our positions, blowing his whistle, leading his men and firing his pistol until he finally died at the rubber tree near my bunker.

I was very impressed with the dedication and determination of this enemy officer. He taught me what leading by example really means. Every time I'm tempted to take some shortcuts and not lead by example, I think of this brave enemy officer and the example he set.

Of course, it's not necessary for us in the corporate world to go to those extremes. However, we must overcome the temptation to take the easy route, instead of leading by example. The rewards of leading by example will pay great dividends in your acceptance and credibility as a leader.

"It is hard to beat a man who never gives up."
Babe Ruth

I had an opportunity to lead by example under fire about three months after the battle described above. I was again commanding my artillery battery on a different fire base at a jungle airstrip near Bu Dop, Vietnam, in the middle of enemy territory. On this occasion, we didn't have an infantry company with us, so there were only about 100 soldiers defending the fire base.

At midnight, we were attacked by a Viet Cong Regiment, which is about 800 or 900 soldiers, supported very effectively by several 60mm mortars. After about a ten-minute mortar barrage on our position, they came out of the jungle about 100 yards away and attacked us across the single runway airstrip. The frontal "kamikaze" attacks continued all night long.

Because the enemy was so close and attacking across an open runway, we lowered our howitzers and fired directly at the attacking soldiers. Normally, artillery weapons fire high in the air to hit targets several miles away. When the attack started, I was in the fire direction bunker along with my boss, a battalion commander who happened to be visiting my battery at the time. The fire direction bunker was dug ten feet in the ground and well protected with sandbags. It was a relatively safe location.

After the attack started, mortar rounds were landing throughout the battery position and bullets were flying everywhere. The battalion commander told me to stay in the bunker, because it was too dangerous to go outside. However, I knew my men were in exposed positions and that I had to go out and lead them in the defense of the fire base. I immediately left the relative safety of the bunker and joined my men in the fight.

As duty required of any leader, I went from howitzer to howitzer during the night, directing and leading my men by example under fire. I was wounded during this attack, but managed to delay medical support until after the battle ended the next morning. I could have stayed in the bunker as ordered by the battalion commander, but it was extremely important that I set the example and lead my men under fire.

Incidentally, I think almost every commander in the Army under similar circumstances would have done the same. I'm convinced that if I'd stayed in that bunker, I could not have continued to be an effective leader in that organization. Again, effective leaders must always lead by example – especially under adverse conditions.

"You must be careful how you walk, and where you go, for there are those following you who will set their feet where yours are set."
Robert E. Lee

Standing in the Door

I spent more than twelve years in paratrooper organizations – 101st Airborne Division, 82nd Airborne Division, and XVIIIth Airborne Corps. In a paratrooper organization, there are at least one or two parachute jumps a month. These jumps involve the entire unit (all ranks) and are normally made under simulated combat conditions. Many of these jumps are made at night.

Jumping from an airplane is not a routine activity, even for the most experienced paratroopers. There's always some fear and concern. Potential disaster, such as a parachute not opening, getting parachutes entangled with another jumper in the air, and injuries from landing on obstacles on the ground are always real possibilities.

The officers and senior non-commissioned officers (sergeants) must always set the example and show bravery during parachute operations in order to gain the respect of the soldiers and help calm their fears of jumping. One very effective way to do this is to be the first person in the aircraft to jump.

Located at each of the two jump doors in an aircraft are a set of lights – one green and one red. At the one-minute-until-jump warning, the red light goes on, which is the signal for the first jumper to "stand in the door." The first jumper actually stands in the open door with his hands touching the outside of the aircraft in preparation for making a vigorous exit from the aircraft.

As you can imagine, standing in this open door for one minute, with the airplane bouncing, seeing the ground flying by a few hundred feet below, and feeling the strong wind in your face, is much more exciting (frightening) than jumping from a position further back in the airplane. For jump positions two and higher, the jumper cannot see the ground or get the sensations the first jumper experiences.

At jump time, each jumper closely follows the jumper in front of them and, as they approach the jump door, they turn toward it and quickly exit the aircraft. This happens so fast that each jumper is at the jump door only a second or less. Jumping from positions two or higher is still a significant event, but it isn't as scary as "standing in the door."

To lead by example, I often "stood in the door," as did other officers and non-commissioned officers. This paid great dividends with the younger jumpers and greatly increased the prestige and credibility of the person who "stood in the door." It's critical for leaders to "stand in the door," and lead by example at every opportunity.

> *"Our greatest glory is not in never failing,*
> *But in rising every time we fail."*
> *Confucius*

Another case of leading by example under fire was in Desert Storm. I was a brigadier general and the Artillery and Rocket Commander of the XVIIIth Airborne Corps Artillery, leading several thousand of our great soldiers. In Desert Storm, the U.S. VIIth Corps (about 150,000 soldiers) attacked the Iraqi positions in Kuwait, and the XVIIIth Airborne Corps made a deep penetration into Iraq to outflank the enemy and hit the Iraqi elite Republican Guard divisions from the flank.

I was in the group that made the deep penetration into Iraq. Our invasion forces were in our attack positions in Saudi Arabia only one mile from the Iraqi border. However, we weren't sure if we were going to attack because of ongoing negotiations with Saddam Hussein. At 10 o'clock one evening, the general officer commanders received a coded message that told us to launch the attack at 5 o'clock the next morning.

My boss, Lieutenant General Garry Luck, the XVIIIth Airborne Corp Commander, knew I liked to "lead from the front." He had told me I shouldn't be with the first units to cross into Iraq and that my position as a general was to be two to three miles behind the front lines with my command headquarters.

Based on these orders, I told my command sergeant major, who traveled with me along with my assault headquarters and bodyguards, that we would not be crossing into Iraq with the initial assault units. Our command headquarters group, which consisted of about four vehicles and twenty men, would cross into Iraq about an hour after the first units attacked.

Morning came and the first of my men and fighting units started the attack across the Iraqi border on schedule. I immediately went to my command sergeant major and said, "Sergeant Major, you've got to really hustle and get our vehicles and people ready to roll fast because I've changed my mind; we're going with the first assault troops."

The sergeant major, who knew me well, said, "Sir, I already knew what you were going to do. We're all ready and loaded, let's go." Clearly he knew me better than I knew myself. He knew I wouldn't be able to watch my soldiers crossing the line unless I was with them. Always lead by example under fire.

> *"You can't build a reputation on what*
> *you are going to do."*
> *Henry Ford*

In summary, leading by example will multiply your acceptance and credibility as a leader more than any other single thing you can do. Never miss an opportunity to lead by example under fire or under adverse conditions. It's definitely worth the extra effort.

Two Cautions about Leading by Example

> *"Example is not the main thing in influencing*
> *others, it is the only thing."*
> *Albert Schweitzer*

If you're not willing to lead by example, you should be honest with yourself and with your organization and not accept a leadership position. In the long term, you and your organization will benefit from your honesty.

If one of the leaders who report to you refuses to lead by example, or is unable to lead by example, change that person's attitude or get a replacement as soon as possible. Our employees deserve good leaders and our organizations will not accomplish their goals without motivated leaders who lead by example.

"The ultimate measure of a man is not where he stands in moments of comfort, but where he stands at times of challenge and controversy."
Dr. Martin Luther King

CHAPTER 9

PROVIDING VISION

"Vision without action is a daydream.
Action without vision is a nightmare."
Japanese Proverb

Every organization looks to its leaders to provide vision. This is one of the key duties of a leader but, unfortunately, based on my experience in corporate America, providing a clear and meaningful vision is often not accomplished very well. The vision isn't just a few "standard" words. It must be a "call to arms" that inspires employees to achieve higher and higher goals. It must be something the employees think is worthwhile.

The vision should not be about monetary goals, making quotas, or increasing shareholder value. It should be more "spiritual or motivating" than the standard business objectives. The vision should be clear, simple, and with no buzzwords. It conveys a reason for your existence. It should not be a long dissertation, but only a few hard-hitting and inspirational words that influence everyone in the organization.

After the vision is determined, briefed, and "sold" to the employees, a series of documents can be developed to go from the general to the specific.

These documents have different names in different organizations, but typically a strategic plan is developed from the vision. From the strategic plan, specific concrete objectives and a mission statement are formed. Then specific goals are developed to support the accomplishment of the vision.

The vision should be clear, simple, and with no buzzwords. It conveys a reason for your existence. It should not be a long dissertation, but only a few hard-hitting and inspirational words that influence everyone in the organization.

"A leader is a dealer in hope."
Napoleon Bonaparte

Examples of Great Vision

In my military experience, the best example of a visionary statement was the Army's previous theme: "Be All You Can Be." This short hard-hitting vision inspired every soldier to reach his or her full potential and thus increase the quality of every military organization. Notice that "Be All You Can Be" is not a monetary goal, and has nothing to do with quotas or shareholder value.

The Army Materiel Command (AMC) also had a great vision statement. The AMC develops and produces the weapons and military equipment for the Army. Its vision statement was, "We Make Great Stuff." This was short, sweet, meaningful, and inspirational.

Some great vision setters in the corporate world have included Lee Iacocca at Chrysler, Jack Welch at General Electric, Sam Walton at Wal-Mart and, of course, Bill Gates at Microsoft. All these leaders had great vision, the ability to inspire their employees to higher and higher levels of performance, and the ability to translate their vision into concrete results.

Importance of Vision

"Would you tell me please which way
I ought to go from here?"
"That depends a great deal on
where you want to get to."
Lewis Carroll, Alice in Wonderland

I've lived in Japan twice, for a total of four years. The first time was with the U.S. Army, working closely with the U.S. Embassy there, and the second time was with Motorola, as its Director of Engineering and Operations. During those tours, I amassed a great deal of experience working with Japanese companies and with their CEOs.

The Japanese fully recognize the extreme importance of vision. In Japan, the CEO or chairman is not involved in the day-to-day operation of the company. The CEO's primary responsibility is to provide the vision for the organization and to inspire the employees with their knowledge and wisdom. CEOs spend much of their time showing their care and concern for the workers and the organization.

In the late 1980s and early 1990s I was a brigadier general in the U.S. Embassy in Korea. One of my major duties was to work with U.S. companies that wanted to do business in Korea. We provided advice to these companies on how to successfully conduct business there. We also helped them with their business plans and made appointments for them with the appropriate Korean government agencies and officials. On many occasions, we would attend these critical meetings.

One very interesting experience involved two competing U.S. companies vying for a multi-million contract to sell the Korean Air Force its next fighter aircraft. The competition was between General Dynamics with its F-16 fighter and McDonald-Douglas with its F-18 fighter. This multi-million dollar deal was very critical to the future of both U.S. organizations.

It was very interesting to see the strategy derived from the vision of each of these companies, and how that strategy was designed to win the competition. General Dynamics' approach was to hire many high-level retired U.S. military and government officials, including several former four-star generals and prominent civilians who had served at the Cabinet level.

General Dynamic's vision was to work from the top of the Korean hierarchy down to the lower-ranking officials. Because almost all Korean senior officials at that time were either active or retired military officers, its plan was to convince the higher Korean officials to favor the F-16, with the expectation that the lower-ranking people would then be ordered to support it.

McDonald-Douglas' vision was quite different. Recognizing that consensus is very important in Asian societies, it planned to work from the bottom up, rather than from the top down. It hired U.S. agents at the "fighter pilot" level (majors, lieutenant colonels and colonels), who then interacted with their counterparts in the Korean Air Force and Defense Department. They felt that if the Korean pilots favored the F-18, then the higher officials would be forced to agree.

Both strategies were effective, but the McDonald-Douglas approach seemed to be the most effective. Its F-18 was initially chosen by the Korean Government, but subsequent lawsuits and investigations in Korea, alleging vice and corruption in the selection process, caused the decision to be eventually reversed, and then reversed again.

Summary

*"The hand will not reach for what
the heart does not long for."*
Welsh Proverb

A clear, concise vision that presents a reason for being and inspires the organization to operate at a higher level is key to its success. The development of this vision is not a human resources function. The highest-level people in the organization must create this vision, with input from all levels of the organization, and then "sell" the vision to every employee.

CHAPTER 10

SAYING "NO" TO THE STATUS QUO

"Great leaders are never satisfied with the current level of performance. They are restlessly driven by possibilities and potential achievements."
Donna Harrison

One of the most dangerous and often repeated sayings in business is, "if it ain't broke, don't fix it." I'm always wary when I hear someone say that, because it's the slogan of people who aren't open to change. It's a call for inaction. People who believe in that saying think the future is going to be like the past and that today's solutions will fit tomorrow's problems.

However, the only sure thing in business or life is that the future will be different than the present, and probably in a totally unexpected way. Therefore, we need leaders who don't accept the status quo, and who are constantly looking into the future and devising new strategies and solutions before the new realities generate serious problems. The

> **The only sure thing in business or life is that the future will be different than the present, and probably in a totally unexpected way.**

military, rightly so in many cases, has often been accused of preparing to fight the last war. This also happens very often in the corporate world because of the prevalent, "if it ain't broke, don't fix it" philosophy.

> *"If the rate of change on the outside*
> *exceeds the rate of change on the inside,*
> *then the end is near."*
> **Jack Welch**

There have been several important times in my career when I didn't accept the status quo. In each case, I had many people telling me, "If it ain't broke, don't fix it." Fortunately, I didn't listen to this bad advice, and the resulting benefits to my organization and my career were significant in every case.

We need leaders who don't accept the status quo, and who are constantly looking into the future and devising new strategies and solutions before the new realities generate serious problems.

The Grenada invasion was discussed in Chapter 6. As you recall, the U.S. forces invaded the island of Grenada because Fidel Castro maintained a large military supply base there, which was being used to support communist insurgencies in several countries in Central and South America. Also, many American students in the medical school there felt threatened by the forces of the newly established communist-leaning Grenada governor.

I was the commander of the artillery forces on Grenada. In the Army, the senior artillery commander has an additional duty as the ground force "fire support coordinator," responsible for making sure the supporting fire from the Air Force, and the Naval gunfire from ships offshore, are coordinated with the Army ground operation.

The U.S. at that time wasn't fully prepared to conduct "joint operations" – operations involving two or more services (Army, Navy, Air Force and Marines). Fortunately, as a result of the lessons learned in Grenada, our ability to conduct joint operations has increased dramatically.

Early in this operation, we were having difficulty getting the Navy ships just off the Grenada shore to fire their powerful and very accurate guns in support of the ground operation. The problem was that we couldn't communicate with the ships, because we didn't know their radio frequencies and codes.

To solve this problem, I got on an Army helicopter to fly out to the Navy ships about two-three miles offshore. My intent was to land on one of their ships and swap radio frequencies and codes face-to-face with my Navy counterparts. The Navy, however, is very particular about unauthorized aircraft – even ones with U.S. markings – landing on their ships, and requires prior coordination and positive radio contact to verbally clear any aircraft to land.

However, I didn't have their radio frequencies, so I couldn't get prior coordination, nor could I establish radio contact to get permission to land. As we approached one of the ships, we were strongly warned over a powerful loudspeaker on the ship that we were not allowed to land. We could also see its big guns turning toward us and a group of Marines pointing their rifles at our helicopter. They couldn't be totally sure who we were but we hoped they could tell we were Americans.

We landed on the ship without permission and were immediately surrounded by people with bad attitudes and guns. After being thoroughly "chewed out" by the ship's captain, we swapped frequencies and codes and solved our mutual communications problem. If I had accepted the status quo and not landed on that ship, the invasion forces would not have had the benefits of naval gunfire for the ground operation.

> ### *"If you do what you have always done, you will get what you have always gotten."*
> ### *Anonymous*

In Desert Storm in Iraq, I again took a big chance by not accepting the status quo. I was the commanding general of many thousands of soldiers in the XVIIIth Airborne Corps Artillery. I was in charge of all artillery and rocket fire for the corps, which consisted of more than 150,000 soldiers. Before we launched the attack, we had several months to develop the plans and strategy we were going to use against the Iraqi army.

Desert warfare has been traditionally characterized by tank battles and artillery duels between the opposing forces. The Iraqi artillery had us outgunned by about three to one in number of artillery weapons on the battlefield. Therefore, our artillery plans and tactics were very important to the outcome of the war. Many American lives could be saved by a great artillery plan aggressively implemented.

One of my best officers — in fact one of the best officers I ever served with: Lieutenant Colonel John Ryneska (later Major General Ryneska) — led a study on the Iraqi artillery tactics and their ability to find or acquire our units as targets. He determined through intelligence reports and analysis that the enemy's ability to find and target our fast-moving units on the battlefield was poor and that the Iraqi artillery would follow their written doctrine exactly.

In addition, they expected us to follow our doctrine to the letter. Since the Iraqi artillery was going to have difficulty finding the location of our artillery units to engage with their guns, they'd probably blindly shoot at the places on the battlefield where we "should be," based on our doctrine. U.S. doctrine calls for our artillery to be positioned about one-third of the range of the particular type of artillery behind the front lines. That is, if the range of a particular artillery weapon was nine miles, we would locate the artillery unit about three miles behind the front lines.

We concluded that the Iraqi artillery would continually fire at locations where our artillery units should be located, based on our doctrine. We then made a bold move and decided to violate the status quo and our long-standing artillery doctrine by keeping our artillery much closer to the front lines.

Because we expected our infantry and mechanized units to move very fast and not get pushed back by the Iraqis, we felt our artillery units would be relatively safe just behind the front lines. I was told by one of our senior generals that this violation of our doctrine had better work or I'd be in serious trouble.

When the war started and we advanced on the enemy, they fired thousands of artillery rounds where they thought our forces would be located. However, the rounds flew over our heads and landed behind us. Not a single American soldier in the XVIIIth Airborne Corps was killed by enemy artillery. Because of the great artillery soldiers and leadership from the officers in the organization, we subsequently destroyed more than seventy-five percent of their artillery without the loss of a single American artillery weapon.

This great achievement was made possible by rejecting the status quo and developing a new plan based on our prediction of how the enemy would operate. The easy solution would have been to follow our doctrine, which had been developed and perfected over many years, based on what happened in the past.

In our corporate organizations, it's extremely important that leaders look into the future and devise solutions and strategies that address and solve future problems.

"In the end, it is important to remember that we cannot become what we need to be by remaining what we are."
Max De Pree

During the period when I was the commander of the 82nd Airborne Division Artillery at Fort Bragg, N.C., I again didn't follow the status quo. The 82nd Airborne Division is composed of approximately 12,000 paratroopers. The Division Artillery which I commanded included all the artillery soldiers in the division – about 2,500 paratroopers.

During a previous tour in the 82nd Airborne several years earlier, we conducted realistic (and dangerous) live-fire exercises with the infantry units of the division, where we fired artillery "danger close," or about 100 meters from the advancing infantry. These exercises trained the various units of the division to work together in live-fire situations very similar to actual combat.

However, I discovered when I returned to the division that these live-fire exercises at some point had been discontinued. I strongly felt it was critical to reinstitute these exercises. It's well-known among experienced combat veterans that a unit in combat fights like it trains in peacetime. Therefore, it was very important to do live fire exercises in peacetime so we'd be prepared in war.

Many officers in the division didn't want to reinstitute these exercises because they were very dangerous. The small margin of error in firing artillery within 100 meters of our soldiers can result in friendly-fire casualties if anyone makes a mistake. Friendly-fire incidents are tragic and have dire consequences for the responsible people.

I had to overcome a great deal of resistance in the infantry community, as well as in the artillery community, to convince people that we needed to restart these important live-fire exercises. Finally, with the great support of the division commander, Major General Ed Trobaugh, we reinstated these critical live-fire training exercises throughout the division. Again, the status quo had been overcome to achieve very positive results for the organization.

However, one caution on changing the status quo. An organization must be very careful about what significant changes it makes, and when it makes them. There are times when you'll be going against a tide that can't be changed. A great amount of energy can be wasted on these "losing battles." It's critical that a leader be able to determine what needs to be changed and what can't be changed. Therefore, change the status quo when appropriate, but do it with great intelligence, and avoid fighting losing battles.

CHAPTER 11

BALANCING CARING AND COMPASSION

"The art of leading, in operations large or small, is the art of dealing with humanity, of working diligently on behalf of men, of being sympathetic with them, but equally, of insisting that they make a square facing toward their own problems."
S.L.A. Marshall, Men Against Fire

Remember the Sun-tzu quote that stated: "If you treat your soldiers like your children, they will follow you to the deepest valleys." It's very important that you genuinely care for the welfare of your people and have true compassion. This isn't something you can successfully fake for a long period of time. Your employees will know whether you really care about them or not.

In the Army, every good commander really cares for his soldiers. In fact, a big part of the selection process is to choose people for leadership positions who have a record of genuinely caring for their people.

Taking care of your people is not a human resources (HR) responsibility – it's a leader's responsibility. The leader of the organization must place his or her "personal stamp" on all programs concerning

91

the care and welfare of the people in the organization. The HR people are very good at implementing and administrating these programs; however, they're your programs. The leader should be very involved and very visible in the implementation of the programs. The employees should clearly feel these programs are the leader's programs, rather than HR-initiated programs.

Harry Truman was a captain in the Field Artillery in World War I. He was a great example of a leader who genuinely cared for his men, but was tough when he needed to be. His promise to his men was very simple but forceful. He told them: "You soldier for me and I will soldier for you."

Excessive Caring and Compassion

"Care is no cure, but rather corrosive.
For things that are not to be remedied."
William Shakespeare
Henry VI, Part I, Act III

The Army is very good at caring for people. However, there are times when the needs of the organization are more important than the needs of the individuals in the organization. One of the biggest mistakes made by many leaders is an excess of compassion for people who will not change, and who insist on doing the same old things in the same old ways. Leaders must not harm the overall organization by being excessively caring for an individual or small group of individuals.

There's a saying in the Army that a leader who shows excessive care for his people will spend ninety percent of his time on five percent of their people. I've seen this happen many times, both in the Army and in the corporate world. Leaders must understand that their time and energy is valuable and that they cannot afford to spend too much time on problem or troubled people.

This is a very difficult concept for many leaders. Some feel a true leader never gives up on any of his or her people. This is a very valid and worthwhile emotion, but it shouldn't be taken to the extreme. Your primary responsibility is to your organization as a whole and not to a few individuals. Therefore, really care for your people, but don't let the organization as a whole suffer because of excessive caring and compassion for a small group of people.

One of the biggest mistakes made by many leaders is an excess of compassion for people who will not change, and who insist on doing the same old things in the same old ways.

As a young major in the 82nd Airborne Division Artillery, I had a commander named Colonel (later General) Vernon Lewis. He was a very, very tough but caring commander. He taught us many lessons, including caring for your soldiers, but he didn't "suffer fools." He also taught us to make a very determined effort to help people become productive members of the organization, but

to put a limit on the time allocated for problem people.

A leader's first obligation is to provide leadership to the organization. Rehabilitating problem
people is a worthy cause but not a leader's primary
responsibility.

My Army career almost ended before it got
started. In the early 1960s, I was a young and very
inexperienced first lieutenant with the First Calvary
Division in Korea. Due to a critical shortage of captains, I was given command of an artillery battery
(about 100 people). Normally, battery commanders
are captains – one rank higher and with many more
years of experience than lieutenants.

I was very excited about getting this command
as such a junior officer. However, in retrospect, I
didn't have the experience or maturity required for
this responsible position. The battery had a few
experienced, dedicated soldiers, but many were
young, drafted, homesick boys who just wanted to
get out of the Army and go home.

I thought I could turn all of these soldiers into
mature, dedicated, hardcore, communist-hating pro-
fessionals. I also thought I could help each man solve
all his personal and financial problems. I spent ninety-five percent of my time on five percent of my
people and, as a result, I wasn't a very good commander. I was very wrong but I didn't realize my
mistake until it was too late.

I was moved to another position in the battalion and got a mediocre Officer Efficiency Rating
(OER) for the battery command position. I thought

my career was over. Normally, when you get a poor OER from a command position, your career goes into a tailspin and you never get promoted again.

However, through hard work and many positive OERs in future command and staff positions, I made the high rank of brigadier general before I retired from the Army. I'm sure many people who knew me in the battalion in Korea were surprised at my eventual success. Being overly caring almost ended my career. I learned the lesson: "care for your people but don't have excessive compassion," the hard way.

In the corporate world, women are often at a disadvantage. Many companies have "good old boys' clubs" that favor the male executives. The men in these clubs sometimes have an advantage with promotions, bonuses, and stock options. I've received benefits by being a member of these clubs. However, I've learned that this excessive caring for the people in a selected group is wrong and harmful to the organization.

These clubs hurt the organization by excluding many very talented and motivated people who could potentially make great contributions. In addition, the morale and loyalty of the people excluded from the clubs are damaged when they observe people in the club getting benefits, promotions, and advantages they clearly don't deserve.

I eventually learned these lessons by being excluded from one of these "clubs." In my last organization, the senior vice president was a very capable woman. However, she supported a group of women executives and employees who openly called themselves, "the Girls' Club." I soon learned how women executives must have felt when confronted with a "good old boys' club."

Payback is sometimes hard. These women had known each other and worked together for several years. They had attended each other's weddings and were godmothers of each other's children, etc., etc. The female senior vice president was very partial to the women in the club. Most of these women were very capable and deserving of their positions. However, several of them performed at very low levels and yet continued to get promotions and have great influence in the organization.

Leaders should go to great lengths to make sure there are no "favorite" groups in the organization that enjoy privileges they don't earn or deserve.

We called these women executives the "Teflon Crew," because nothing bad ever stuck to them. This taught me a lesson I'll never forget. It's very wrong and harmful to the organization to favor a particular group. Leaders should go to great lengths to make sure there are no "favorite" groups in the organization that enjoy privileges they don't earn or deserve.

Summary

A leader should genuinely care for his or her people but not to the extent where the entire organization is harmed. Leaders should not spend the majority of their time on an individual or small group of problem people. If a reasonable attempt to rehabilitate, retrain, or motivate these people fail, then they should be moved to more suitable positions or separated from the organization.

In addition, leaders should not allow exclusive "clubs," or play favorites. Leaders must be fair, even-handed, and impartial in dealing with their employees.

CHAPTER 12

MAKING DECISIONS ON LIMITED INFORMATION

"Be willing to make decisions, this is the most important quality in a good leader."
General George Patton

There's a principle in the military that a decision made in a timely manner and executed vigorously is better than the perfect decision made too late. Commanders in combat situations are required to make life-or-death decisions based on only ten to twenty percent of the needed information. This so called "fog of war" exists because of the fast-moving and unpredictable conditions in a combat zone.

There's also a "fog of war" in the corporate world, where changing customer demands, competitor actions, and marketplace changes make the timely collection of information very difficult. Leaders do have a great need for information in order to make the proper decisions, which is very understandable. However, one of the biggest mistakes made by military and corporate leaders is delaying key decisions because they insist on having more complete information.

A note of caution: the key for a wise leader is to be able to determine when a decision must be made. The ability to make this determination requires great experience, insight, and perhaps a "sixth sense." However, know when to be cautious. Rash decisions can also be harmful to the organization. In some cases, no decision is better than a bad decision.

One of the biggest mistakes made by military and corporate leaders is delaying key decisions because they insist on having more complete information.

"The early bird may catch the worm, but the second mouse gets the cheese."
Unknown

Critical Decisions with Limited Information

When we launched the attack into Iraq during Desert Storm, we had very limited information about the enemy. We weren't sure how many enemy forces were in front of us, or exactly where they were located. We were also very unsure about whether or not the roads and open desert were heavily mined with anti-tank and anti-personnel mines.

The initial tactics by the Iraqis were also unclear – would they fight us on the border, or would they retreat, inflicting casualties on our troops as we advanced? Would they use chemical weapons? As we crossed the line, we had to be prepared for any eventuality, and make life-or-death decisions on the spot. Much to our surprise, there were very few mines on the road or in the desert, and no chemical weapons were used against our forces.

Similar conditions confronted our commanders in Vietnam. In the jungles, the situation was always very unclear, yet we had to make instantaneous decisions with perhaps five percent of the information we needed.

I was a brand new second lieutenant in the 101st Airborne Division at Fort Campbell, Kentucky during the Cuban Missile Crisis in the early 1960s. The U.S. had detected Soviet missiles installed in Cuba targeting our mainland. In addition, we detected several Soviet ships suspected of carrying additional missiles en route to Cuba.

The U.S. demanded that the missiles be dismantled and that the Soviet ships return to Russia. President John F. Kennedy and Soviet Premier Nikita Khrushchev were on the brink of the world's first nuclear war. It was clearly the most dangerous time in the Cold War.

The American military was secretly told to prepare to invade Cuba. At one point, we were given a specific D-Day and told to issue live ammunition and make the final preparations to conduct a paratrooper assault near Havana as part of a large U.S. invasion force. I was assigned to help plan the parachute assault.

However, we had very limited intelligence information on the size, strength, and location of the Cuban forces. In addition, we were forced to plan our parachute operation in an area with vast sugar cane fields. We were concerned that the Cubans would diagonally slice the sugar cane stalks with machetes in such a way as to make them into sharp "daggers" that would injure or kill our jumpers as they landed.

However, we had been given the orders to go, so we had to make many decisions with very little information. Our expectation was that our great commanders and dedicated soldiers would find a way to make our plan work, regardless of the real situation on the ground. In extreme situations, leaders must make decisions based on the best information they have, and then be prepared to live with those decisions.

> **In extreme situations, leaders must make decisions based on the best information they have, and then be prepared to live with those decisions.**

Examples of Not Making Critical Decisions

One of the most disappointing experiences in my military career was the poor performance of the French Foreign Legion Battalion attached to the XVIIIth Airborne Corps in Desert Storm. Before the attack against Iraq, we trained with this battalion in the deserts of Saudi Arabia and were very impressed with their military bearing, knowledge, skills, and attitude. They looked and sounded like a first-class military organization. We were so certain they'd be great in combat that we made them one of the lead organizations in the attack across the Iraqi border.

My command group crossed the Iraqi border

near the middle of the French Foreign Legion Battalion formation. Once we started the attack and were taken under fire by the Iraqis, the French Battalion proved to be a very poor organization. They were very slow to advance or make any tactical decisions until they had a great deal of information about the enemy. In contrast, the American forces were much more aggressive and just "rolled over" any Iraqi opposition.

The French forced our units to slow down to keep from forming gaps in our lines. After the first day, we moved them off the front lines and assigned them a backup or reserve role. They seemed very happy to be out of the line of fire.

This is a good example of the dangers of not making necessary decisions because of a lack of information. A normally highly qualified organization became ineffective because its leaders would not make decisions with only limited information available to them.

I also encountered a similar situation in my corporate life when I was in Prague in the Czech Republic, a former Communist block country with a very poor mobile telephone system. I was the Czech Republic Country Operations Director for Motorola, in charge of forming an organization and putting in place a country-wide digital mobile telephone system from scratch.

The Czech government was our official customer, but our real customer was a German company – Deutch Telecom. Since there were no experienced digital telephone people in the Czech

Republic, Deutch Telecom was hired as an operations company to run the Czech system on behalf of the Czech government.

The German executives were very efficient and intelligent, but wouldn't make decisions until a tremendous quantity of information was collected and correlated. To get any decision from the German executives required many beers, plus an overwhelming amount of data, charts, and graphs.

However, the contract with the Czech government required that we activate different parts of the system not later than specified dates, or face serious monetary penalties. In many cases, we desperately needed decisions from the Germans in order to keep on schedule. These decisions were often delayed, causing us to work 18-hour days, amassing statistics that in many cases weren't critical to the decision under consideration.

This was the epitome of "paralysis by analysis." Fortunately, we made our schedules without penalties, but the reluctance of the Germans to make critical decisions at key times made the accomplishment of our contract almost impossible.

"Too often we measure everything
and understand nothing."
Jack Welch

I also had a tour with Motorola in Japan, where I was its Director of Operations and Engineering. I found the Japanese customers were also reluctant to make any business decisions until an overwhelming quantity of information was amassed and analyzed. They would often require the presentation of information that wasn't significantly related to the decision being considered.

In many cases, this delay in decision making resulted in situations where we had to "cut corners" in order to meet our schedules and avoid penalties. Often, a less perfect decision made in a timely manner would have given us time to accomplish the required engineering tasks much better. Their executives also had "paralysis by analysis."

I've found in my military and corporate life that a good decision, not the perfect decision, but a good decision made in a timely manner and aggressively executed, is much better than the perfect decision that's made too late, because someone waited to get all the possible information. It's best to make a good decision at the key time, and update and fine tune the decision as the situation dictates.

I had a great boss in Motorola, Jack Scanlon, who would give us a "data termination date." At some critical point in the decision making process, determined by the savvy leader, you must take the available information and make a decision. If you wait until you have 100 percent of the possible information, some of the initial information you had is now probably outdated.

1. The information we have is not what we want.
2. The information we want is not what we need.
3. The information we need is not available.
Finagle's New Laws of Information

The French Foreign Battalion and the German and Japanese customers I worked with would have achieved much better results if they had made critical decisions at key times and executed those decisions aggressively. I've seen battles lost in both the military and corporate worlds by delaying critical decisions. Good leaders don't allow the battle to be lost by overanalyzing the problem.

CHAPTER 13

RIGHT UNLESS PROVEN WRONG

"The aircrews will win the war despite the plan from higher headquarters."
The Strategic Air Command Aircrew Theorem

This principle is violated routinely in our society – we do it backwards. In most organizations, headquarters is considered to be right and the field wrong, unless proven otherwise. More than ninety-five percent of the organizations I've seen in both the military and corporate worlds truly believe the ultimate truth resides in their headquarters.

Leaders should routinely and consistently solicit opinions from the operational people in the field who are actually face-to-face with the customers.

Instead, leaders should routinely and consistently solicit opinions from the operational people in the field who are actually face-to-face with the customers. This is normally the best possible source of information for leaders and executives at headquarters.

One of the biggest dangers for a leader is when

people in the field stop providing their opinions because they feel those opinions are being ignored or not highly valued. Staff executives at headquarters are critically important to any organization, but their primary role should be to support the operational people in the field – not direct their activities. However, staff executives usually exert great influence, partially because they're usually physically co-located with the senior leaders and are in a good position to "get their ear" and thus win their confidence.

Listen primarily to the people who make the money, rather than the ones who count the money.

Another way to state the correct principle is: listen primarily to the people who make the money, rather than the ones who count the money.

Examples of Headquarters Right – Field Wrong

My last job in the corporate world was with an international telecommunications company headquartered in Minnesota. This company was the extreme example I've seen of headquarters always being considered right and the field wrong. On numerous occasions, the regional vice presidents and general managers (I was the Midwest VP and General Manager) would receive an unexpected telephone conference call from the senior vice president at headquarters and be notified of a major policy change or new strategy. The regional managers would then be asked to give their approval to the new policies or strategy on-the-spot.

Normally, the regional general managers in the field would not be aware that the policy or strategy was under review, nor did they have any opportunity to give input into the final decision. Those general managers who didn't immediately approve the new policy or strategy were labeled troublemakers. This is an extreme case, but similar stories abound throughout the corporate world.

In the military, the primary example of the violation of this principle was the Vietnam War. The decision making at the national level in this war could not have been worse. This was a prime example of the people back in the headquarters (Washington and the White House) thinking they had all the answers. Policy, strategy, targets, and rules of engagement at the tactical level were dictated by a group of executives in Washington, who had little knowledge of what the realities were in the field.

The Secretary of Defense during much of this period, Robert McNamara, was, in my view, particularly inept and uninformed. He consistently failed to listen to advice that was contrary to his predetermined views. Unfortunately, this situation was made worse by many of our senior military commanders at the time, who accepted and implemented numerous bad policies that led to us losing the war.

When headquarters doesn't listen, it's the responsibility of the field leaders to aggressively and forcefully inform the senior leaders of the realities in the field – even if it's detrimental to the field leaders' careers.

Example of Field Right – Headquarters Follows

Desert Storm was just the opposite of Vietnam, in that the leaders in Washington solicited the views of the commanders in the field and incorporated those views into the development of policies and strategies. I credit the Chairman of the Joint Chiefs of Staff, General Colin Powell, for this almost perfect balance between the political and military realities.

We did fail to achieve our goal of ending the Saddam Hussein regime, by concluding the war too early.

However, the war was run very effectively up to that point. The generals and the colonels actually fighting the battle in Desert Storm were considered to be right, and headquarters at the Department of Army, the State Department, and the White House all listened and incorporated the views from the field commanders into the plan. That was a stark contrast with Vietnam.

When I was assigned to the U.S. Embassy in Korea in the late 1980s, the Ambassador was James Lilly, who earlier had been Ambassador to China. He was a very good leader, who always operated on the principle that the people on the cutting edge where the action is taking place have information that's critical and correct, unless proven otherwise. He listened attentively to the people in field positions and valued their input and recommendations.

His embassy staff, which was comprised of many very able Foreign Service officers, followed the Ambassador's lead and worked very closely and in harmony with the field operatives on all issues. The

RIGHT UNLESS PROVEN WRONG 111

leadership atmosphere created by Ambassador Lilly was a model for others to follow.

Caution

Creating and maintaining the atmosphere where the field is right and headquarters is wrong will require constant emphasis from the leader of the organization. The "natural" state of affairs will be just the opposite. However, the benefits will be very positive for the organization. If the field people feel they're being ignored or that their opinions aren't valued, there's a great danger that they'll stop talking to headquarters. At that point, that organization is in very, very big trouble because it's "flying blind."

CHAPTER 14

BUILDING ON STRENGTHS

"The growth and development of people
is the highest calling of leadership."
Harvey S. Firestone

It's very important in the corporate world, as well as in the military, that we build on people's strengths, and not spend too much time trying to improve their weaknesses. This is contrary to the "conventional wisdom" in many organizations.

I've been in several organizations in the Army and in the corporate world that go to great lengths to identify and "correct" the weaknesses of each executive. This is normally done by corporate HR specialists, using elaborate questionnaires and interviews with peers, subordinates, and senior executives. Each evaluated executive also takes a battery of personality tests and leadership questionnaires.

All these results are then correlated to determine the weaknesses of each executive. The next step is to devise and implement a program to correct these weaknesses by reading the right books, going to the right schools, reflecting on your weaknesses and progress, etc. This is normally followed by interviews with HR people or senior executives every ninety days, to make sure all weaknesses are being corrected.

I'm not totally against these programs. We all

have weaknesses and it's certainly a good idea to try to correct them. However, we spend far too much time doing that, rather than developing strengths. Unfortunately, it's been my experience that most people, as hard as they might work to correct their weaknesses, fall back into their old habits after a few weeks or months.

We should spend much more time building and developing people's strengths, and not so much time trying to correct their weaknesses.

We are who we are, and it's almost impossible to change us into something different. We should spend much more time building and developing people's strengths, and not so much time trying to correct their weaknesses. The organization can then, when feasible, adjust the job responsibilities to capitalize on each person's strengths. The organization will be much better and the employees more efficient and satisfied.

The corporate world is in a much better position than the military to adjust jobs to each person's strengths. In the military, job positions and descriptions are about ninety-nine percent fixed. People are fit into these jobs, rather than the jobs being formulated to capitalize on people's strengths. This is an area where the military could learn from the corporate world.

Develop People

*"The ultimate leader is the one who is willing
to develop people to the point where they
eventually surpass him or her in
knowledge and ability."*
Fred A. Manske, Jr.

There's an old American Indian story that teaches leaders a critically important lesson about identifying and developing good people.

An Indian brave was walking along the plains one day and saw an eagle egg on the ground. He knew he couldn't climb the high cliff and put the egg back in the eagle's nest, so he put it in a prairie chicken's nest. The egg hatched and the prairie chickens accepted the eagle as one of their own. The eagle grew up as a prairie chicken, never knowing he was really an eagle.

One day, the prairie chickens saw this magnificent eagle with a six-foot wingspan flying and soaring high overhead. All the prairie chickens, including the eagle who thought he was a prairie chicken, looked in awe at this magnificent, wonderful sight. The eagle in the prairie chicken's nest said, "I have big wings, wouldn't it be wonderful if I could fly high overhead like the eagle?"

The prairie chickens' leader laughed and reminded the eagle that he was a prairie chicken and would never soar like an eagle. Unfortunately, the eagle believed it, and remained on the ground with the other prairie chickens for the rest of his life.

It's important for every leader to realize there are "eagles" in every organization, hidden among the prairie chickens. It's the responsibility of leaders to identify and develop these eagles to their full potentials. These "eagles" will eventually "soar like eagles" and be key members of the organization. Good leaders don't allow eagles to remain in the prairie chicken nests.

> *"As we look ahead into the next century, leaders will be those who empower others."*
> **Bill Gates**

Develop Leaders
One of the most critical responsibilities of every leader is to develop other leaders at all levels.

> *"It's not the leader's job to create followers; it's their job to create leaders."*
> **Jack Welch**

In every organization, leaders should be evaluated and judged by how successful they are in developing other leaders. In the Army, this is considered very critical. The reputations of senior military leaders are often greatly enhanced by the success of leaders they trained and mentored.

This is also prevalent in the world of sports. For example, in the National Football League, there are several famous coaches who are held in very high esteem because they developed others who eventually became successful head coaches.

Clearly, in the sports world and in the military world, leaders who develop other successful leaders are held in very high esteem. However, I've found this isn't always true in the corporate world. In fact, I've seen many cases where senior executives didn't want to develop leaders, because they were concerned that their protégés might surpass then in the organization.

> **Corporations should have programs to recognize, honor, and reward leaders who develop other effective leaders.**

It takes a very secure leader to overcome these concerns and openly develop other strong leaders. Corporations should have programs to recognize, honor, and reward leaders who develop other effective leaders.

Training

Training is essential to developing people. When I was in Motorola, training was a very high priority. Each employee was required to attend forty hours of training per year. Managers were required to make sure that each of their employees actually attended the required forty hours and that the courses they took were appropriate to their position and responsibilities.

The Army has a similar program in most organizations. This investment in training pays great dividends. Employee are not only better qualified in their jobs, but also feel the organization cares about

As a minimum, each leader – at all levels including the CEO – should have at least two weeks of leadership training per year.

their future development.

Extensive leadership training for leaders is a must. As a minimum, each leader – at all levels including the CEO – should have at least two weeks of leadership training per year. In my view, to ensure credibility, this leadership training should be presented by people who have actual leadership experience, and not those simply with academic degrees.

Don't Bother Good Performers

> *"Don't tell people how to do things.*
> *Tell them what to do and let them*
> *surprise you with their results."*
> **General George S. Patton**

The surest way to "turn off" a good performer is through micromanagement. Over supervising and excessively controlling a good employee stifles initiative and greatly harms morale. I learned this lesson from experience, and from the writings of General George Patton of World War II fame.

In the movie "Patton"- starring the great actor George C. Scott – General Patton gave a famous address to the soldiers of the 3rd Army just before they were committed to combat in Germany. The speech was very candid, inspiring, and patriotic.

However, it was not politically correct by today's standards, due to some tough language and some profanity. I recommend you download the speech from the Internet and read the unedited version.

In one part of the speech, General Patton told about an incident in North Africa that taught him not to bother good performers. In March 1943, he was leading the U.S. II Corps in North Africa against the Nazi's best commander, General Erwin Rommel, known as the Desert Fox. During one of the gigantic tank battles, things were not going well for the Americans. The outcome of the battle was very much in doubt.

General Patton, as usual, was leading the attack near the front lines of the battle. Enemy artillery was landing everywhere, the German tanks were firing their main guns in a deadly barrage, bullets were flying, and the Nazi fighter aircraft were strafing the American forces. The situation was critical.

General Patton tells the story that, as he was moving forward near the front lines of the battle, he drove past a fifteen-foot high telegraph pole near the road. At the top of the pole was an American soldier working on a telegraph wire. General Patton couldn't believe that this soldier was at the top of that pole with enemy fire all around. The general stopped his vehicle in the middle of the attack and asked the young soldier why he was up that pole? The soldier calmly said, "Sir, there's a wire that needs fixing, and my job is to fix wires."

There's a great lesson in his words. If your job is to fix wires, and there's a wire that needs fixing, you should fix it, even under bad conditions and even when your boss isn't watching.

General Patton was very impressed and said, "Soldier, all these bullets are flying around, artillery is landing nearby, and enemy planes are strafing this road. Doesn't that bother you?" The soldier looked down and said, "Not as much as you do, sir." The clear object of the story is that you shouldn't bother people who are doing their job.

Caution

"Don't get buried in the thick of thin things."
Stephen R. Covey

Leaders who micromanage and over-supervise greatly hinder the development and morale of their employees. In addition, under an over-controlling leader, the organization will work at only a fraction of its capacity, productivity, and efficiency.

Micromanagement might produce short-term gains in some situations, but it will greatly impair the effectiveness of your organization in the long term.

Leaders should not micromanage, but they must pay attention to detail and closely monitor the operations. Continually checking and monitoring the operations is not micromanagement. A very popular Army saying I've found is 100 percent true is: "An organization does best those things that the boss checks." Therefore, make many checks, but don't get involved in the details of the operation unless it's absolutely necessary.

CHAPTER 15

BEWARE OF "YES" PEOPLE!

"The people to fear are not those who disagree with you, but those who disagree with you and are too cowardly to let you know."
Napoleon Bonaparte

This is a short but very important chapter. Each of us – including leaders – naturally values other people who think like us, look like us, and act like us. If people are like us, they must be intelligent, wise and well informed.

Notice that many up and coming executives in an organization are remarkably similar to the senior leaders. We all naturally want employees and subordinate leaders who make us feel comfortable and who basically agree with our brilliant decisions. In short, we don't want to admit it, but we're very comfortable with yes men or women. Leaders must overcome these natural feelings.

In all the key positions I held in the military and corporate worlds, I've always purposely hired several people with contrary views and the courage to express those views. Some of these people even jokingly have called themselves the "designated naysayers." These people sometimes made me frustrated and uncomfortable, but they were among the most valuable people in the organization.

When I was the Czech Republic Country Director for Motorola, one of the first people I hired was a head project manager – a retired Marine Colonel - I had worked with previously. He was very qualified but he didn't hesitate to disagree with me and strongly present a contrary view. I think he took pleasure in making me feel uncomfortable from time to time, but he forced me to consider alternative views that sometimes led me to adopt a solution different from my initial thoughts.

We must have people in our organization who have contrary views and who feel free to openly question our decisions. Without them, the organization will stagnate, because everyone will have very similar views, and new programs and ideas will be difficult to implement. However, these people won't speak up unless the leader creates the proper atmosphere. Don't be like the executive who said:

> *"I don't want yes men around me.*
> *I want everyone to tell the truth,*
> *even if it costs them their jobs."*
> **Samuel Goldwyn, Hollywood Producer**

Leaders should take a very close look at their senior staff executives. This is a prime location for "yes men." They're probably isolating you from many key realities in your organization. They're also probably "no men" to the remainder of the organization.

Some people, in jest, don't agree with this concept.

"I only have 'yes' men around me.
Who needs 'no' men?"
Mae West, Exotic Dancer

Perhaps Mae had a different agenda than most corporate leaders. A real corporate leader said it best:

"If you have a yes person working for you,
one of you is redundant."
Barry Rand, former Xerox CEO

In today's competitive marketplace, no executive wants to be thought of as redundant.

You'll sometimes think people who tell you things you don't want to hear are unintelligent, irritating, obstructionists, and negative thinkers. They must simply not understand the situation and are just flat wrong. However, it's critical that you put your ego "on hold" and hire people with contrasting views, and have them be an integral part of all your decision making processes.

CHAPTER 16

LONELY AT THE TOP

*"A no uttered from the deepest conviction is better than a yes merely uttered to please.
Or what is worst, to avoid troubles."*
Mahatma Gandhi

One of the first lessons you learn as a leader is that every decision you make will be unpopular with some people in the organization. There are very few perfect decisions everyone will embrace as brilliant. Don't let negative views keep you from making good decisions. Don't be deterred by the doubters.

Normally, in life and in business, there are several alternatives, all of which have some downside. Not every decision is good for all employees. Leaders must make decisions based on the facts, the situation, and what's best for the organization, and let the "chips fall where they may."

Leaders must make decisions based on the facts, the situation, and what's best for the organization, and let the "chips fall where they may."

"I cannot give you the formula for success,
but I can give you the formula for failure,
which is —try to please everybody."
Herbert Bayard Swope

Don't make the mistake many leaders make — making decisions that please the most people or offend the least number of people. Also, don't lower your standards in making hard decisions. Decisions based on these concepts are almost always bad ones. You're not selected as a leader in order to be popular or to lower standards, but to lead the organization in the proper direction, even if it's not always the easy way for the employees or the organization.

> **You're not selected as a leader in order to be popular or to lower standards, but to lead the organization in the proper direction, even if it's not always the easy way.**

Popular or Respected

"When you're going through hell —
Just keep on going."
Winston Churchill

Leaders must not be overly concerned about being popular. This is very difficult for many leaders, because we all have a basic human need to be liked. The age-old question for leaders is: Do you want to be popular, or do you want to be respected? Of course, we want to be both, but many times that's not possible. In that case, it's much better to be respected than popular.

If you're respected by your employees, they'll be more likely to accept hard decisions as tough, but fair and reasonable. They'll understand your decisions were made for the good of the organization and not for personal gain. They might not like the decisions you're making, but they'll respect them.

Leadership is Lonely

"Be who you are and say what you feel,
because those who mind don't matter
and the ones who matter don't mind."
Dr. Seuss

Leadership is a very lonely job. Some degree of loneliness is an unavoidable consequence of effective leadership. In several surveys with senior leaders, about one-third of the respondents said that loneliness was the most negative consequence of being a leader. Incidentally, nearly half said that putting up with backbiting and bitchiness is the worst thing about being a leader.

For leaders to be effective in the long term, they need to recognize that they'll be lonely, and acquire skills to counter those negative feelings.

Examples

Leadership is often a lonely job, because leaders must make hard decisions and then personally face the possibly dire political and morale consequences of those decisions. After Desert Storm, I was appointed by the Chief of Staff of the Army to be the official investigating officer for a deadly friendly-fire incident that took place during one of the nighttime tank attacks on the second night of the war.

In this incident, an American tank unit attacked another American unit they mistook for Iraqis. One soldier was killed and others wounded in the attack. Being the investigating officer in an incident where one American soldier accidentally kills another is a very difficult and "gut-wrenching" job.

The purpose of conducting an investigation in these cases is to find out exactly what happened, so procedures can be adapted to prevent similar incidents in the future. In addition, the investigating officer must determine if anyone should receive any type of punishment – to include court-martial actions – for their role in the incident.

The eventual findings of the investigating officer are a classic no-win situation. If the investigating officer finds no one is guilty because everyone acted reasonably, based on the uncertain and confusing conditions on every battlefield – the so-called Fog of War – then many people in the Army and the media will say the Army "whitewashed" or "covered-up" wrongdoing.

However, if you rule that some soldiers are guilty of wrongdoing, then there'll be people in the Army and media who say the Army is sacrificing a few innocent soldiers as scapegoats. This is a classic lose-lose situation for the investigating officer.

In this very emotional and politically charged atmosphere, the investigating officer must make a decision based on the facts of the case, the conditions at the time, the overall combat situation, and the degree that the "fog of war" was a factor. The investigating office must make the right decision and have the courage to withstand the barrage of criticism that's sure to follow. This is a very lonely position. As Harry Truman said, "the buck stops here."

In Chapter 10, I discussed the decision I made in Desert Storm to deviate from the standard artillery doctrine and position our attacking artillery units much closer to the front lines than our doctrine specified. This was a very difficult and dangerous decision. If I was wrong, it would be paid for with the lives of my soldiers. I would undoubtedly be held fully responsible for the consequences. Fortunately, I was correct and the decision saved lives and was a factor in our eventual defeat and destruction of the Iraqi artillery.

> *"In matters of style swim with the current,*
> *In matters of principle, stand like a rock."*
> **Thomas Jefferson**

Leadership is definitely lonely and can make you unpopular. However, leaders must make difficult decisions that potentially have great costs for the organization, and be prepared to take the consequences. Being a leader is a lonely job. However, as salespeople say, "It goes with the territory." If you're not ready and willing to make these tough decisions and accept the consequences, then you're not ready to be a leader.

One important line in the Cadet Prayer at West Point is, "Give me the strength to choose the harder right instead of the easier wrong." This should be the guiding principle for all leaders. Make the proper decisions and then take the consequences for those decisions, even if they're unpopular.

CHAPTER 17

LEADERSHIP CHALLENGES/ FINAL OBSERVATIONS

"No amount of study or learning will make a man a leader unless he has the natural qualities of one."
Sir Archibald Wavell
London Times, Feb. 17, 1941

Leadership is one of the most challenging and rewarding activities you'll ever experience in life. Leadership is a calling similar to teaching or being in the clergy. However, it's not true that everyone can be a good leader, just as everyone can't be a rocket scientist, or a major league pitcher, or an astronaut. Natural ability plays a part.

There are leadership principles that can be learned and perfected and, through hard work and good leadership training, you can become a better leader. However, some people are simply better leaders than others, regardless of the training and effort expended.

Some people who are very gifted, talented,

> **There are leadership principles that can be learned and perfected and, through hard work and good leadership training, you can become a better leader.**

intelligent, and ambitious are not cut out to be good leaders. People who have a great need to seek control and wield power are normally not good leaders. However, if you have the basic talent, the dedication, the willingness to serve, the motivation to develop your leadership skills, and feel the calling – you can be a good or even a great leader. Be true to yourself and your organization; if you don't want to make the sacrifices required of a leader, seek other legitimate and fulfilling endeavors.

Have Fun

"The business of life is to enjoy oneself."
Norman Douglas
An Almanac

The final advice I have for you as leaders is to lead a balanced life – work hard, play hard, and spend time with your family. In addition, surround yourself with people who also have a balanced view of life. Workaholics are doomed to an unhappy, unfulfilled life.

> **The final advice I have for you as leaders is to lead a balanced life – work hard, play hard, and spend time with your family.**

I learned this lesson late in my career from a very unexpected source. During one very interesting period, I was Motorola's Country Operations Director in Prague, Czech Republic. Our task was to design, construct, and operate a country-wide digital telephone system from scratch for the Czech Republic government. I had employees from nine countries – a mini United Nations. Several of my key managers were Germans.

We were scheduled to activate the first portion of the cellular system on a Monday morning in July. This was a very important date because we were subject to substantial monetary penalties if we failed to activate on schedule. I had a meeting with all my managers about a week before the critical date to make sure we'd be ready.

I emphasized that we were slightly behind schedule in several critical areas and that we needed to work day and night until we were sure we were ready. We worked very hard that Monday through Friday, but there were many final tasks and checks that needed to be made over the weekend, in order to be ready for the very critical Monday system activation.

When I came to work early Saturday morning, everyone was there except for the three German managers. I was told they'd departed for their previously planned weekend activities. I knew about those plans but I thought, based on our meeting, that everyone understood we were all required to work through the weekend. Of course, the American managers had cancelled their weekend plans and came to work bright and early.

Fortunately, we successfully activated the system on Monday morning as planned, and didn't have to pay any penalties. When the German managers returned, I called them into my office to find out why they went on their weekend vacations rather than work during those final two crucial days before the system activation. One of the German managers explained their reasons. His explanation changed my entire outlook on life.

He told me that life is like a three-legged stool. For that stool to stand, all three legs had to be strong. The first leg of that stool was the work leg. People should take their jobs very seriously and work hard to foster their own careers and do everything they can to make their company a success. It was very important to have a very strong work leg of the stool.

The second leg of the stool was the activity or hobby leg. He said everyone should have one or more outside activities, whether it be golf, jogging, hockey, tennis, stamp collecting, or any other interesting activity. People should pursue their chosen activities vigorously so they have a strong second leg of the stool – the hobby or activity leg.

The third leg of that stool was the family leg. People should make sure they spend quality time with their families on a regular basis in order to have a very strong family leg. If a person (the stool) has a strong work leg, a strong hobby or activity leg, and a strong family leg, the stool will stand. If any of these legs are weak or missing, the stool will eventually fall.

I completely understood the explanation and learned a very valuable lesson from an unexpected source. Unfortunately, I learned this lesson too late to apply those principles to the first thirty years of my working life. Therefore, my advice to you is to work hard, play hard, and spend time with your family.

Follow this advice and your "stool" will always stand when others all around you are falling.

Final Thoughts

I call upon all of you to dedicate yourselves to being good leaders and, when appropriate, good followers. If your team wins, then everybody wins.

Be yourself. Don't try to fool your people and yourself with a phony "corporate" personality. People will eventually see through this façade.

> *"O what may man within him hide,*
> *though angel on the outward side."*
> *William Shakespeare*
> *Measure for Measure, Act III, Scene II*

Remember that soldier General Patton encountered on the telegraph pole in combat in North Africa. That soldier taught us two great lessons. First, if a wire needs fixing and it's your job to fix wires, then fix it to the very best of your ability, even if you weren't told to fix the wire, or if no one is watching, or even if you won't get credit for the job. Secondly, if your employees are doing their job, don't bother them or attempt to micromanage.

Remember the Indian story about the eagle in the prairie chicken nest. There are eagles in your organization disguised as prairie chickens. It's your responsibility as a leader to identify these "eagles" and develop them to their full potential.

Leadership is a very difficult task but it's enormously satisfying. Successfully leading a group of people to achieve great accomplishments, whether in combat or in a corporate environment, is the ultimate high. I wish you all the best in your leadership endeavors.

ABOUT THE AUTHOR

Brigadier General Nick Halley (U.S. Army, Retired) is a recognized expert on leadership and terrorism. He has commanded thousands of our soldiers in combat in three conflicts – Vietnam, Grenada, and Desert Storm. He is an army paratrooper, army ranger and special operations veteran. He has been awarded many significant decorations, including two Silver Stars for bravery in combat actions, four Bronze Stars, and two Purple Hearts for wounds in combat operations.

In addition to his combat commands, General Halley has had a wide variety of assignments, including assistant professor of mathematics at West Point, assignments to the U.S. embassies in both Korea and Japan, and many years with the Army's premier fighting division – the 82nd Airborne Division.

His final active duty assignment was the Commanding General of the XVIIIth Airborne Corps artillery and rocket forces in Desert Storm, where he commanded tens of thousand of our soldiers in the most challenging leadership environment – combat. Since his retirement from the Army, General Halley has had a distinguished civilian career at the director/vice president/general manager level with several prestigious international electronics firms, including Motorola.

General Halley is a graduate of the United States Military Academy at West Point, and holds a master's degree in nuclear physics from the University of Virginia. Currently, he is the on-air military and terrorism expert for WGN-TV in Chicago, which is seen nationwide on cable.

TO ORDER BOOKS

Books can be ordered for $16 directly from the author at:

Telephone: 847-719-2637
Email: nickhalley@msn.com
Website: www.generalnickspeaks.com

The book can also be purchased through Amazon at www.amazon.com

Bulk discount rates are also available by contacting General Halley by telephone, email or through his website.